The Biblical Seminar
46

PEACE, VIOLENCE AND THE NEW TESTAMENT

D1522003

PEACE, VIOLENCE

AND THE **NEW TESTAMENT**

Michel Desjardins

Sheffield Academic Press

To Adrien and Simon

Copyright © 1997 Sheffield Academic Press

Published by
Sheffield Academic Press Ltd
Mansion House
19 Kingfield Road
Sheffield S11 9AS
England

Typeset by Sheffield Academic Press
and
Printed on acid-free paper in Great Britain
by Cromwell Press
Melksham, Wiltshire

British Library Cataloguing in Publication Data

A catalogue record for this book is available
from the British Library

ISBN 1-85075-799-2

CONTENTS

PREFACE

The inspiration for this book came from my students at the University of Toronto (1987–92). They first asked the questions (e.g., 'What is this violence doing in the New Testament?'), then were forthcoming with their thoughts (e.g., 'The parables feel liberating'; 'As a lesbian I find myself continually assaulted by my own sacred texts') and patient with me over the years as we worked carefully through the primary texts, gradually developing their ideas and mine into a coherent whole. The students' names should rightfully fill the front cover of this book. I can only hope that they are not too disappointed with the final outcome, and that with this study in hand others also will be able to experience at least some of the intellectual excitement we had in those years.

I also owe a great deal to those who generously took the time to read the manuscript in its various incarnations, and who offered kind words and helpful suggestions. I think in particular of Bill Arnal, Willi Braun, Scott Brown, Bill Burrows, Theo de Bruyn, Tony Burke, Ken Derry, David Griffiths, Paul Hartford, Barry Henaut, David Jobling, Sol Nigosian, Peter Richardson, Larry Schmidt, Marty Shukster, and Philip Tite.

And I remain deeply grateful to Ellen, my life partner, for her support and inspiration.

Michel Desjardins
Department of Religion and Culture
Wilfrid Laurier University

Chapter 1

INTRODUCTION

> For I am knowledge and ignorance.
> I am shame and boldness.
> I am shameless; I am ashamed.
> I am strength and I am fear.
> I am war and peace.
>
> I am the one who is honored,
> and the one who is praised,
> and the one who is despised scornfully.
> I am peace,
> and war has come because of me.[1]

Christianity presents itself as a religion of peace, and support for this claim is strong. Throughout the world, the churches' prayers, sermons and songs resonate with 'peace'. Christian individuals (e.g., the Berrigans), denominations (e.g., the Mennonites) and groups (e.g., Project Ploughshares) openly lead the way in the anti-war movements. There is also an underlying Christian core to many peace-promoting individuals and groups. Consider Greenpeace. Originally founded in response to the American nuclear weapons tests in Alaska, this group was established in accordance with the Quaker form of protest known as 'bearing witness', which involves going to the scene of an objectionable activity and registering opposition to it simply by being there. This Quaker connection is the Christian basis of two long-lasting Greenpeace beliefs: direct action is crucial for effecting change, and this action must be nonviolent—even when one is faced with violence.

---

1. *The Thunder: Perfect Mind* 14.26-32; 18.20-25. This work comes from the collection of documents discovered in Egypt in 1945. It is a revelation discourse with a female figure speaking in the first person. For introduction and translation (by G. MacRae), see *The Nag Hammadi Library in English* (Leiden: Brill, 3rd edn, 1988 [1977]), pp. 297-303.

The Christian preoccupation with peace is grounded firmly in the New Testament. Direct references to 'peace' abound and are dispersed in all but one of the New Testament's 27 books. The 13 Pauline letters all open with 'peace' in their greetings. More important still is the centrality of 'peace' in several key New Testament books. For instance, the heart of Ephesians is the call to peace between Jews and non-Jews, based on the author's understanding of Jesus (2.14-17).[2]

> For he is our peace; in his flesh he has made both groups into one and has broken down the dividing wall, that is, the hostility between us... So he came and proclaimed peace to you who were far off and peace to those who were near.

As well, Jesus, through certain actions (e.g., his concern for the woman caught in adultery—Jn 8.2-11), sayings (e.g., 'love your enemies'— Mt. 5.44) and parables (e.g., the Good Samaritan—Lk. 10.29-37), is portrayed as sensitive to the issue of peace and violence. Indeed, exhortations to lead peaceful lives abound in the New Testament. These references go a long way toward explaining Christianity's ongoing concern for peace.

There is another side to the issue. We all know of Christians and Christian leaders who have instigated, condoned, or participated in wars. The crusades in the Middle Ages waged against the Muslims in the name of Christ remain imprinted on our minds. So too does Christian anti-Semitism, which has existed from Christianity's inception, only to peak horrifically in the middle of this century. And the continuing violence between Protestants and Catholics in Northern Ireland reminds us that Christian-backed violence has not disappeared. Correspondingly, the American rhetoric about the 'godless' communist empire has been part of the justification for the arms race and the Cold War—indeed, some Christian fundamentalists in America still actively support increased militarization with a view to bringing on the end of this world and the beginning of God's new age.

Christian involvement in violence is also firmly grounded in the New Testament. One could in fact argue that at times it is the New Testament itself which leads Christians to violence. Some of this support is direct. Jesus' entrance into the temple, according to the Gospel of John (Jn 2.13-15), suggests that even Jesus at times condoned violence:

---

2.   All Bible quotations are taken from *The Holy Bible, New Revised Standard Version* (New York, NY: Oxford University Press, 1989), with permission.

> The Passover of the Jews was near, and Jesus went up to Jerusalem. In the temple he found people selling cattle, sheep, and doves, and the money changers seated at their tables. Making a whip of cords, he drove all of them out of the temple, both the sheep and the cattle. He also poured out the coins of the money changers and overturned their tables.

Some of the textual support for Christians acting violently is less direct. Just as 'peace' at times is understood broadly to include social justice, for instance, or inner harmony (the New Testament writers would add: a direct relationship to God through Jesus), so too does 'violence' include far more than a physical component. Here I might note the New Testament writers' tendency to denigrate others, both inside and outside the group. Paul, for one, can wish castration on some Christians who do not agree with him (Gal. 5.12), death (or ostracism) to an incestuous member of his community (1 Cor. 5.3-5) and damnation on others (Gal. 1.9). Matthew, for his part, tars the Pharisees with a single brush: in his eyes they are all wicked and damnable. John does likewise with 'the Jews', and more—professing them to be intrinsically evil: 'You are from your father the devil' (8.44). These types of exhortation abound throughout the New Testament, contributing significantly to its violent side.

The tension in the New Testament Scriptures themselves between advocating peace and condoning violence presents the interpretive challenge out of which my study emerges. I am unable to reduce the evidence either to one option, 'the New Testament is fundamentally peace-promoting', or to the other, 'the New Testament encourages people to be violent'. The strong presence of both is striking and intriguing.

What also fascinates me is my own curiosity with the topic, and the perspective I bring to the material. Three factors may serve as possible explanations. All emerge from the society and the academic communities in which I have lived since beginning university over 25 years ago.

The North American preoccupation with peace and violence during the last half century is the first factor. To be sure, these concerns have always been part of the human condition. Since 1945, however, the continuing threat of global nuclear annihilation has added a heightened sense of urgency to humanity's violent outbreaks and inclinations, sparking an unimaginable growth of weapons as well as a considerable number of peace movements. The threat of a world-destroying conflagration has hung over my head since childhood. I have also been immersed in the growing domination of the media, which have sub-jected me to daily barrages of violence from around the world—the broader the definition of violence, the more of it there is to read and to see. I am a child of this age, and its violence in particular has marked me deeply.

The second formative factor has been the gradual change in my society's understanding of 'peace' and 'violence' to include, but also extend beyond, the physical realm. 'Violence against women', for instance, is now seen to be more than rape and wife-battering. It also involves discrimination in the workplace and, for some at least, an attitude that all women are by nature best suited to raising children. A modern North American definition of violence now includes two complementary aspects. First, violence is an overt physical destructive act carried out by individuals or countenanced by institutions. This is still what normally comes to mind when one speaks of 'violence', and a violent act of this nature ranges from a slap to murder. Second, vio-lence is also a personal or institutional act which, as Robert McAfee Brown aptly puts it, 'violates the personhood of another in ways that are psychologically destructive rather than physically harmful'.[3] In this sense, one can speak of pornography as 'violence against women', and government inaction on 'Third World' debt as 'structural violence against the poorer nations'. This second type of violence for many of us has come to be as real and as dangerous as the first. Moreover, the two work hand in hand. The same points can be made about 'peace', which increasingly is seen to incorporate both the absence of violence and genuine concern for the physical, social and psychological well-being of others.

Non-physical types of peace and violence cannot be delimited with precision. Physical violence, for instance, can be recognized and measured by all. But what may be 'psychologically destructive' for one person (e.g., being told that, as a woman, you must stay home and obey your husband) may not be so to another. Brown's definition of violence rings true in a late twentieth-century North American con-text, yet accepting it means giving up the possibility of arriving at a specific understanding of violence that is shared by all. To mention only one example: I may consider the insistence that women appear veiled in public to be a 'violation of personhood', but many men and

---

3. Robert McAfee Brown, *Religion and Violence* (Philadelphia, PA: Westminster Press, 2nd edn, 1987 [1973]), p. 8.

women, for instance, would have good reasons for disagreeing with me. Still, the benefits of including non-physical components in the discussion of peace and violence far outweigh the risks, and I intend to do so in this study. The result is a broad and fluid definition of peace and violence, which includes a wide range of actions, attitudes and relationships, and to a considerable extent reflects my own views and those of the society in which I live.

Broadening 'peace' and 'violence' in this manner has important repercussions on how one understands the New Testament message. First, it encourages us to approach these texts with a different perspective than the writers had. To be sure, first-century Jews and Christians were concerned with structural inequities and discrimination against others, but they did not call this 'violence'. They also lived in a world not as influenced by secularism. What they would have considered their deepest understanding of peace—good relations between humans and God, which leads to eternal life—holds less interest for many of us now in Europe and North America. It is also not my concern. Applying a modern understanding of peace and violence, then, as I do in this study, does not result in the determination of the first-century Christian view, but in the assessment of these ancient texts by modern criteria. Second, a broader, more secular understanding of these terms results in the emergence of more 'violence' from the New Testament. Limiting 'peace' and 'violence' to the physical realm, the New Testament, especially when compared to other sacred scriptures such as the Hebrew Bible, the Qur'an and the Bhagavad Gita, has long stood out positively as advocating non-violence toward others. Accordingly, scholars and believing Christians have justifiably emphasized the peaceful characteristics of the New Testament teachings. Allowing violence to range beyond physical limits considerably changes that picture.

The academic training I have received, including my continuing involvement in a university department of religious studies, is the third factor that has moulded my perspective. The academic study of religion, as practised in the latter part of this century, is based on the premise that interpreters, regardless of their own religious beliefs, can—indeed must—distance themselves from the texts and traditions under examination. The purpose is to understand rather than judge, and to focus on the human elements of religion in the social contexts in which they arise. The existence of God, for instance, or the truth claims of any particular group, cannot be proven empirically, so they are kept out of the discussion. They are not taken for granted. The academic approach to the New Testament naturally leads to different results than those of practising theologians or other Christians, who believe that the New Testament is divinely inspired and that God is fundamentally peace-promoting and loving. These Christian presuppositions lead to the conclusion that the New Testament must be advocating peace. When I set out on this study several years ago, my intent was not to prove that the New Testament, in its heart of hearts, is a peace-promoting collection of the highest order; nor, for that matter, was it to prove the opposite. I sought to understand what occurs when one approaches these texts from an academic perspective, applying a modern understanding of peace and violence to them. My intent now is to share with others the results, which I find unusual and challenging.

The ideal reader whom I had in mind while writing this book is someone who has little familiarity with the New Testament, but is willing to explore it through an academic lens; someone who is deeply concerned about peace and violence; and someone who enjoys struggling with ethical and philosophical issues. Some Christians, especially those not previously exposed to the academic study of religion, may take offence at what they perceive to be an anti-religious stance. All I can say on this matter is that I do not intend to offend or scandalize. I would hope that devout Christians could also read this book with gain. Some non-Christians, however, may not be all that interested in, or favourably disposed to, the New Testament. To those individuals I would say: examine what is in these documents before rejecting them outright, and at least recognize their continuing importance in shaping our European and North American culture. The academic approach to the New Testament is only one way of understanding this literature, but it deserves to be heard by Christians and non-Christians alike. Some New Testament scholars might be surprised that I have not provided a 'historical-critical' reading of these texts, i.e., that I have not consistently put them in their historical and literary contexts or fully engaged the wealth of academic resources concerned with elucidating the New Testament. To my colleagues I would say: what you will see in this book is an approach to the texts grounded in what I have repeatedly encountered from non-academic readers of the Bible. This is a book that only an academic would write, but it is not one that an academic would normally write.

My ideal reader is also someone who is willing to put on two sets of glasses when reading the New Testament. With the first I intend to explore the peace-promoting elements in these documents (Chapter 2); with the second, the violence-promoting elements (Chapter 3). I expect all readers to be more favourably disposed to reading the texts through only one of these lenses. The challenge will be to keep the glasses separate and keep them both on long enough to see reality clearly through their lenses. In closing (Chapter 4), I examine some of the implications.

Chapter 2

PEACE IN THE NEW TESTAMENT

Throughout the New Testament, Christians are encouraged to be peaceful. This chapter highlights the most important elements of that message of peace. It proceeds from the general to the specific. I begin by discussing the uses of the term 'peace' and presenting an overview of some of the New Testament's most notable non-violent exhortations and actions. Then I turn to four components which strongly reinforce a message of peace: Matthew's Sermon on the Mount, the parables attributed to Jesus, the pervasive focus on the imminent demise of the world, and Paul's distinctive ethical stance. Taken together, these help to underline the significant role played by peace in the New Testament.

1. *The Vocabulary*

To note all the references to 'peace' in the New Testament and examine their usage is not the most effective way of exploring the topic, but it remains a good starting point. There are one hundred explicit references to peace in the Greek text. The noun *eirene* (peace) occurs 92 times, the verb *eireneuein* (to live in peace, be in peace, keep the peace) four times, the adjective *eirenikos* (peaceable, peaceful) twice, the verb *eirenopoiein* (to make peace) once, and the noun *eirenopoios* (peacemaker) also once.[1] The number of references is striking, as is

---

1.   The key terms and locations are as follows (all are taken from the 26th edition of Nestle-Aland's *Novum Testamentum Graece*):

a) *eireneuein* (to live in peace, be in peace, keep the peace): Mk 9.50; Rom. 12.18; 2 Cor. 13.11; 1 Thess. 5.13 [4×];

b) *eirene* (peace): Mt. 10.13, 13, 34, 34 [i.e., twice in one verse]; Mk 5.34; Lk. 1.79; 2.14, 29; 7.50; 8.48; 10.5, 6, 6; 11.21; 12.51; 14.32; 19.38, 42; 24.36; Jn 14.27, 27; 16.33; 20.19, 21, 26; Acts 7.26; 9.31; 10.36; 12.20; 15.33; 16.36; 24.2; Rom. 1.7; 2.10; 3.17; 5.1; 3.6; 14.17, 19; 15.13, 33; 16.20; 1 Cor. 1.3; 7.15; 14.33; 16.11; 2 Cor. 1.2; 13.11; Gal. 1.3; 5.22; 6.16; Eph. 1.2; 2.14, 15, 17, 17; 4.3; 6.15, 23; Phil. 1.2; 4.7, 9; Col. 1.2; 3.15; 1 Thess. 1.1; 5.3, 23; 2 Thess. 1.2; 3.16, 16; 1 Tim.

their distribution, for the words occur in every New Testament book except 1 John. Also striking is the preference shown for the noun over the verb form, and, upon closer examination, the significant proportion of occurrences in the Pauline corpus: 29 in the seven undisputed letters (Romans, Galatians, 1–2 Corinthians, Philippians, Philemon, 1 Thessalonians) and 18 in the other six (Ephesians, Colossians, 1–2 Timothy, Titus, 2 Thessalonians).[2] Only Luke's Gospel comes close to this number, with its 14 uses of *eirene* (compared with a single use by Mark, and four by Matthew in only two verses). These references to peace are impressive but not overwhelming. Placing this usage in perspective, the word group for love (*agapan*, to love; *agape*, love; *agapetos*, beloved) occurs in the New Testament 319 times, distributed in every book, and fairly evenly between noun and verb. Still, the high frequency of 'peace' in the New Testament makes the concept stand out even to the casual reader.

What do the New Testament writers mean when they refer specifically to peace? Paul's writings can be taken as representative. He begins every letter with a peace wish. The composite picture that emerges from his letters is that peace is a gift from God, which results in the breaking down of some of the divisions between God and

1.2; 2 Tim. 1.2; 2.22; Tit. 1.4; Phlm. 3; Heb. 7.2; 11.31; 12.14; 13.20; Jas 2.16; 3.18, 18; 1 Pet. 1.2; 3.11; 5.14; 2 Pet. 1.2; 3.14; 2 Jn 3; 3 Jn 15; Jude 2; Rev. 1.4; 6.4 [92×];

c) *eirenikos* (peaceable, peaceful): Heb. 12.11; Jas 3.17 [2×];
d) *eirenopoiein* (to make peace): Col. 1.20 [1×];
e) *eirenopoios* (peacemaker): Mt. 5.9 [1×].

2. Thirteen letters in the New Testament claim Paul as their author in their opening verses. Given their striking differences, scholars have long wondered whether Paul himself could have been responsible for all of them. It was common among Jews in the first century to write in other people's names (usually in order to write as these people would have written had they been alive). Books from that time still exist, for instance, written in the name of Moses, Adam and Enoch, so some of Paul's letters could easily have been authored by others, probably after his death. This possibility, of course, cannot be proven one way or the other, but a scholarly consensus has arisen which puts seven of Paul's letters in the 'undisputed' or 'authentic' category and relegates the others to the 'disputed' or 'deutero-Pauline' camp. Given the nature of my study, I do not often distinguish formally between the two groups of letters. I call them all 'Pauline'. But when I present a distinctively Pauline perspective, the supporting evidence will (as it must) come first from the undisputed letters. Furthermore, since Acts definitely was not written by Paul, its perspective on Paul must be considered secondary.

humans, and between humans themselves. At times 'peace' means 'eternal life'. An example of this is Rom. 8.6: 'To set the mind on the flesh is death, but to set the mind on the Spirit is life and peace' (so also Rom. 2.10; 5.1). Other times Paul refers to an inner state of tranquillity that anticipates eternal life. As part of his closing remarks to the Romans he states: 'May the God of hope fill you with all joy and peace in believing, so that you may abound in hope by the power of the Holy Spirit' (15.13; see also Gal. 5.22). And quite often Paul uses the term to mean a significant reduction in the strife between humans—simply put, getting along harmoniously with others (which he would have linked to the Christians' new relationship with God). One example occurs in Rom. 12.18: 'If it is possible, so far as it depends on you, live peaceably with all'. Another occurs in Col. 1.19-20: 'For in him [Christ] all the fullness of God was pleased to dwell, and through him God was pleased to reconcile to himself all things, whether on earth or in heaven, by making peace through the blood of his cross.' This last reference suggests that 'peace', for Paul, often meant the absence of violence—physical or otherwise (see also Rom. 14.19; 1 Thess. 5.13; Rom. 7.15; 16.11; 1 Tim. 2.1-2). The same is true for the writers of the other New Testament books.

2. *An Overview of the Non-Violent Exhortations and Actions*

A non-violence thread runs through the books that make up the New Testament. This fact is worth highlighting, in spite of the danger that accrues from trying to find uniformity in what is, in many respects, a disparate collection. On one issue at least the New Testament message is clear and consistent: faced with the threat of physical violence, Christians must not reciprocate, even to the point of death. Moreover, Christians are encouraged to avoid instigating violence, and to do all they can to defuse potentially violent situations. These ideals are meant to be realized through a significant personal transformation. What follows in this section is an examination of this ideal as manifested in the New Testament presentations of Jesus, Paul, and Simon Peter (the 'founding fathers'); as expected from the second generation of Church leaders; and as taught to all Christians.

a. *The Founding Fathers*
Jews in Jesus' day had long had a tradition of popular military leaders. King David's autonomous rule (c. 1000–960 BCE) was fondly

remembered, and hopes were kept alive after centuries of foreign domination for another chosen 'son of God' to emerge in David's mould. Two centuries before Jesus, a small group of Jews sparked a revolt against Syrian domination and influence, and the victory that ensued from what came to be called the Maccabean revolt rekindled a glorification of past Jewish military might. The tale of how Mattathias and his sons surprised the Syrian occupying forces and eventually regained control of the temple in 164 BCE was often told in the first century. It lived on in the yearly feast of Hannukah and in the four books of the Maccabees, which enjoyed considerable popularity in Jesus' day. Throughout the remainder of the second century before the birth of Jesus, and much of the first, military expansion of Israel's borders and its area of influence occurred regularly. In the century following Jesus' death, Jews would wage three wars against Roman rule, each of which proved disastrous for them (66–73; 115–117; 132–135 CE). In the last of these, the revolutionaries were led by Bar Kosibah (or Bar Kochba, the 'Son of a Star', as he was nicknamed by Rabbi Akiba, one of the Jewish leaders of his day), an individual who was acknowledged by many to be the Messiah. In this turbulent and revolutionary context, the New Testament presentations of three overtly non-violent Jewish religious leaders, including Jesus, is quite remarkable.

i. *Jesus*. Jesus' life and teachings, at least as it is recounted by the evangelists, reinforce a physically non-violent image. With few exceptions (to be explored in the following chapter) the Gospels present Jesus as a peaceful man who, in spite of growing harassment and violent confrontations, remains calm and does not physically respond to the hostility of outsiders or the treachery and bungling of his followers. He confronts others with words, arguments, and signs, not physical force,[3] and encourages his followers to do likewise. Moreover, when a confrontation ensues he often leaves the scene until people calm down or until he feels the time is right to return.

His attitude toward the Roman and Jewish authorities as well as the people who would make him king are instructive. He does not resist physically—although he may be seen to resist in other ways. When confronted with the question of paying taxes, both to the Romans (Mk

---

3. This non-physical type of confrontation, of course, can still be violent. I will examine that perspective in the next chapter.

12.13-17; Mt. 22.15-22; Lk. 20.20-26) and to the Jewish temple authorities (Mt. 17.24-27), Jesus does not overtly encourage civil disobedience or rebellion. However, his acceptance of social outcasts, such as prostitutes and tax collectors, coupled with his denunciations of the rich and of established social institutions such as the family, reveals a dissatisfaction with the shape of his society.

The Gospels also depict him acknowledging a special relationship with God. John's Gospel especially brings Jesus onto the human stage as a man-God figure at a time when a military messiah was expected. Yet in Jn 6.15, Jesus refuses to let the crowds make him king by force. His kingly entry into Jerusalem (Mk 11.1-10; Mt. 21.1-9; Lk. 19.29-38) is not accompanied by a contingent of armed followers, but is on the back of a colt. Zech. 9.9 is meant to come to mind: 'Rejoice greatly, O daughter Zion! Shout aloud, O daughter Jerusalem! Lo, your king comes to you; triumphant and victorious is he, humble and riding on a donkey, on a colt, the foal of a donkey.' Jesus is the messiah, the evangelists insist, but he is a humble, non-military messiah who does not conquer through physical force. Despite being critical of the social and political structures of his day he does not preach armed revolt.

The story of his arrest reinforces the point. This incident is one of the few recounted in roughly the same manner in all four Gospels.[4] An overall non-violent tenor can be appreciated in the four versions below, especially the strong plea for non-violence in Matthew's version of the story.

> Mark 14.43-50
> Immediately, while he was still speaking, Judas, one of the twelve, arrived; and with him there was a crowd with swords and clubs, from the chief priests, the scribes, and the elders. Now the betrayer had given them a sign, saying, 'The one I will kiss is the man; arrest him and lead him away under guard.' So when he came, he went up to him at once and said, 'Rabbi!' and kissed him. Then they laid hands on him and arrested him. But one of those who stood near drew his sword and struck the

---

4.   Matthew, Mark, Luke and John all narrate the story of Jesus' life and teachings, focusing almost exclusively on the events immediately preceding his death. Each Gospel presents the story differently; John's presentation is particularly distinctive. It is rare for all four Gospels to narrate the same incident or saying, let alone in roughly the same manner. Nevertheless, the first three 'Synoptic' Gospels are remarkably similar in the content and ordering of the events—so much so that their stories can be 'viewed together' (*synoptesthai*) in parallel columns.

slave of the high priest, cutting off his ear. Then Jesus said to them, 'Have you come out with swords and clubs to arrest me as though I were a bandit? Day after day I was with you in the temple teaching, and you did not arrest me. But let the scriptures be fulfilled.' All of them deserted him and fled.

Matthew 26.47-56
While he was still speaking, Judas, one of the twelve, arrived; with him was a large crowd with swords and clubs, from the chief priests and the elders of the people. Now the betrayer had given them a sign, saying, 'The one I will kiss is the man; arrest him.' At once he came up to Jesus and said, 'Greetings, Rabbi!' and kissed him. Jesus said to him, 'Friend, do what you are here to do.' Then they came and laid hands on Jesus and arrested him. Suddenly, one of those with Jesus put his hand on his sword, drew it, and struck the slave of the high priest, cutting off his ear. Then Jesus said to him, 'Put your sword back into its place; for all who take the sword will perish by the sword. Do you think that I cannot appeal to my Father, and he will at once send me more than twelve legions of angels? But how then would the scriptures be fulfilled, which say it must happen in this way?' At that hour Jesus said to the crowds, 'Have you come out with swords and clubs to arrest me as though I were a bandit? Day after day I sat in the temple teaching, and you did not arrest me. But all this has taken place, so that the scriptures of the prophets may be fulfilled.' Then all the disciples deserted him and fled.

Luke 22.47-54
While he was still speaking, suddenly a crowd came, and the one called Judas, one of the twelve, was leading them. He approached Jesus to kiss him; but Jesus said to him, 'Judas, is it with a kiss that you are betraying the Son of Man?' When those who were around him saw what was coming, they asked, 'Lord, should we strike with the sword?' Then one of them struck the slave of the high priest and cut off his right ear. But Jesus said, 'No more of this!' And he touched his ear and healed him. Then Jesus said to the chief priests, the officers of the temple police, and the elders who had come for him, 'Have you come out with swords and clubs as if I were a bandit? When I was with you day after day in the temple, you did not lay hands on me. But this is your hour, and the power of darkness!' Then they seized him and led him away, bringing him into the high priest's house.

John 18.1-12
After Jesus had spoken these words, he went out with his disciples across the Kidron valley to a place where there was a garden, which he and his disciples entered. Now Judas, who betrayed him, also knew the place, because Jesus often met there with his disciples. So Judas brought a detachment of soldiers together with police from the chief priests and the

Pharisees, and they came there with lanterns and torches and weapons. Then Jesus, knowing all that was to happen to him, came forward and asked them, 'Whom are you looking for?' They answered, 'Jesus of Nazareth.' Jesus replied, 'I am he.' Judas, who betrayed him, was standing with them. When Jesus said to them, 'I am he', they stepped back and fell to the ground. Again he asked them, 'Whom are you looking for?' And they said, 'Jesus of Nazareth.' Jesus answered, 'I told you that I am he. So if you are looking for me, let these men go.' This was to fulfil the word that he had spoken, 'I did not lose a single one of those whom you gave me.' Then Simon Peter, who had a sword, drew it, struck the high priest's slave, and cut off his right ear. The slave's name was Malchus. Jesus said to Peter, 'Put your sword back into its sheath. Am I not to drink the cup that the Father has given me?' So the soldiers, their officers, and the Jewish police arrested Jesus and bound him.

In each version of the story Judas appears on the scene with an armed party, and Jesus' followers attempt to prevent his arrest. In the process, one of them (identified as Simon Peter only in John's Gospel) pulls a sword and cuts off the ear of the high priest's slave. Jesus makes it clear that he disapproves of this approach and of an armed arrest, since God intends for him to die: 'Shall I not drink the cup which the Father has given me?' (Jn 18.11). Resisting God's plan is futile, and the time has come for him to be arrested in order to fulfil his destiny. Matthew adds (26.53) that, should Jesus want to defend himself, God would easily take care of matters; Jesus does not need human protection. John has Jesus make the same point to Pilate somewhat later in the narrative (18.36): 'My kingdom is not from this world. If my kingdom were from this world, my followers would be fighting to keep me from being handed over to the Jews. But as it is, my kingdom is not from here.' The underlying message in all four versions of the story is that violence is ineffective in altering God's control over human history. If God had wanted Jesus to escape arrest, the weapons of the arresting party would have done them no good and the weapons of Jesus' followers would not have been needed. 'Submit yourself to God and recognize his plan' might be the story's motto: attempting to interfere with God's plan, especially by violence, is useless.

There are two disruptive features to this common story's peace-promoting perspective. The first is Jesus' apparent lack of concern for the victim. Luke addresses this issue. His Jesus not only rebukes the assailant but heals the victim's ear, reinforcing his plea: 'No more of this!' (22.51). The second problem is that violence *per se* does not appear to be condemned, only violence not in accord with God's plan. Matthew addresses this problem by having Jesus say to the assailant: 'Put your sword back into its place, for all who take the sword will perish by the sword' (26.52). The statement is unequivocal: violence, used to attack others or to protect oneself, is not countenanced by God. Matthew's version of the arrest accentuates most pointedly what is already a non-aggressive image of Jesus.

Jesus' death reinforces this image of non-aggression. Jesus is called 'our peace' by Paul (Col. 1.20), who considers Jesus to have reconciled humanity to God through his own death, not the deaths or killing of others. Jesus' bloody fate, inflicted by the Romans in the most barbarous manner possible at the time—and since then represented by the symbol of violence, the cross—makes a powerful statement for someone, we are told, who could have resisted physically but chose not to do so. Victory is achieved through accepting, not inflicting, violence.

Mark's Gospel elaborates on this image. Through its literary theme of the disciples' misunderstanding, this Gospel effectively transmits the message that Jesus' messianic nature did not involve inflicting violence on others or gaining political control. In this regard, Mark depicts progressively worsening relations between Jesus and his disciples. He paints a bleak picture with broad brushstrokes, insisting that Jesus' non-violent messianic stance was not only misunderstood but strongly resisted by those closest to him. Mark's portrayal of Jesus and his disciples merits some discussion.

The disciples in Mark's Gospel initially appear eager but unperceptive. From 1.16 to 8.26 two characteristics emerge. The first is that Jesus' small band of followers enjoys a privileged position with their teacher, as one might expect. Immediately following his baptism by John the Baptist (or 'the baptizer' as Mark prefers to call John in the opening chapters), Mark has Jesus choose his disciples (1.16). In 3.13-19 he formally appoints the inner group of twelve, and we are given their names. Soon thereafter (6.7-13) he sends them off on a mission on his behalf, having given them the authority to preach and the power to heal and exorcize demons. Despite their privileged position, and their exposure to countless miracles by Jesus, the disciples remain surprisingly unperceptive. Indeed, the attentive reader or listener begins to notice that something is amiss. In the midst of a storm, for instance, the disciples do not call out for the sleeping Jesus to intercede (4.35-41); rather, they appear dismayed and exhibit no faith in Jesus' ability to save them. 'Teacher', they cry out at last, 'do you not care if we perish?' In 5.25-34, when Jesus encounters a woman who has been haemorrhaging for years and perceives her surreptitious touch, the disciples are incredulous that Jesus can recognize one person's touch over another's. Their unperceptiveness continues when Jesus is said to feed more than five thousand people with five loaves of bread and two fish (6.30-44), and then walks across the water to join the disciples who have left the miraculous meal and are now in a boat. These two scenes end with 6.51-52: 'And he got into the boat and then the wind ceased. And they were utterly astounded, for they did not understand about the loaves, but their hearts were hardened.' Mark reinforces this view of the disciples in 8.14-21:

> Now the disciples had forgotten to bring any bread; and they had only one loaf with them in the boat. And he cautioned them, saying, 'Watch out— beware of the yeast of the Pharisees and the yeast of Herod.' They said to one another, 'It is because we have no bread.' And becoming aware of it, Jesus said to them, 'Why are you talking about having no bread? Do you still not perceive or understand? Are your hearts hardened? Do you have eyes, and fail to see? Do you have ears, and fail to hear? And do you not remember? When I broke the five loaves for the five thousand, how many baskets full of broken pieces did you collect?' They said to him, 'Twelve.' And the seven for the four thousand, how many baskets full of broken pieces did you collect?' And they said to him, 'Seven.' Then he said to them, 'Do you not yet understand?'

The disciples are made to look foolish in this episode (and Jesus not all that patient). Understanding only partially, they are like the blind man in the next story (8.22-26), who, when healed by Jesus, at first exclaims: 'I see people, but they look like trees, walking.'

Unperceptiveness changes to misconception in 8.27–14.9, when Jesus' non-violent nature is misunderstood and resisted by his disciples. This section begins with what appears to be a startling about-face, for Peter suddenly declares Jesus to be the Messiah—or 'Christ' in Greek (8.27-30):

> Jesus went on with his disciples to the villages of Caesarea Philippi; and on the way he asked his disciples, 'Who do people say that I am?' And they answered him, 'John the Baptist; and others, Elijah; and still others, one of the prophets.' He asked them, 'But who do you say that I am?' Peter answered him, 'You are the Messiah.' And he sternly ordered them not to tell anyone about him.

Jesus' challenge in 8.21, 'Do you not yet understand?' seems met by Peter in 8.29 ('You are the Messiah') and confirmed by Jesus when he charges the disciples to keep this information to themselves. Yet a problem immediately ensues. Jesus responds to Peter's confession with the first clear prediction of his passion: 'Then he began to teach them that the Son of Man must undergo great suffering and be rejected by the elders, the chief priests, and the scribes, and be killed, and after three days rise again. He said all this quite openly' (8.31-32). Peter takes Jesus aside and rebukes him for speaking nonsense, and Jesus replies: 'Get behind me, Satan! For you are setting your mind not on divine things but on human things' (8.33). With this exchange Mark dramatically begins to show that Peter's understanding of messiahship is not the same as Jesus'.

For Mark's Jesus, messiahship is to be understood only in terms of suffering and death. He redefines this messianic role not once but three times in separate passion predictions which undergird this section of the Gospel (8.31; 9.31; 10.33). In addition, Mark has the heavenly voice call attention to this point in 9.7: 'This is my Son, the Beloved; listen to him!' Still the disciples do not listen: they do not understand and do not accept. They are portrayed not only as unperceptive but as subscribing to a type of messiahship and discipleship at variance with that advocated by Jesus.

Mark repeats this message, lest his audience be as unperceptive as the disciples. Immediately after the second passion prediction the disciples become involved in a discussion about their own merits. Jesus chides them, insisting that discipleship involves a commitment to servanthood: 'Whoever wants to be first must be last of all and servant of all' (9.35). Following Jesus' third passion prediction James and John become embroiled in a similar controversy over prestige and power (10.35-45), and Jesus must again indicate that, just as non-aggression is his path, servanthood and at times even martyrdom must be the path taken by his followers.

What we have, then, in the central part of Mark's Gospel, are three clear passion predictions, followed by a divine confirmation of Jesus' message about his fate, and two scenes of blatant misunderstanding by the disciples. Mark's narrative structure allows us clearly to perceive the direction of his thought.

Mark's way of framing the anointing story in 14.3-9 effectively depicts a further deterioration of the disciples' relations with Jesus, leading from misunderstanding to rejection.[5] The framing verses (14.1-2, 10-11) are as follows:

> It was two days before the Passover and the festival of the Unleavened Bread. The chief priests and the scribes were looking for a way to arrest Jesus by stealth and kill him; for they said, 'Not during the festival, or there may be a riot among the people.'

> Then Judas Iscariot, who was one of the twelve, went to the chief priests in order to betray him to them. When they heard it, they were greatly pleased, and promised to give him money. So he began to look for an opportunity to betray him.

What makes Judas Iscariot betray Jesus, according to Mark's narrative structure, occurs between these two scenes. It is his frustration with Jesus' reaction to the woman who anoints him. According to the story a woman pours ointment on Jesus valued at the modern equivalent of about six months of wages for a blue-collar worker. Jesus understands the gesture as replacing the anointing he will not receive after his death, and explains this to the disciples around him. But they cannot get over the fact that he could allow this amount of ointment to be poured on him, partly because they still have not understood that he is soon to die. They continue to expect him to lead them to political control of the land. Their misunderstanding leads to a lack of sensitivity to his plight, and eventually—due to Judas' action—to Jesus' arrest.

Mark proceeds to emphasize how this rejection is not limited to Judas alone. It is shared by all the disciples. Peter and the others are said to remain oblivious to Jesus' distress in the Garden of Gethsemane before his arrest (14.32-42), not even staying awake to watch with him. After Jesus' arrest, 'all of them deserted him and fled' (14.50). Only Peter remains behind, but even he denies Jesus (in the famous cockcrowing scene), rounding out what amounts, in Mark, to a complete rejection of Jesus and his messiahship by his closest followers. Peter's last words in this Gospel—for that matter, the last words of any disciple here—are pathetically ironic. They are aimed at the bystanders who are attempting to link him with Jesus because of

---

5. This 'sandwiching' technique is typically Markan. Note, for example, how he slips 5.25-34 between 5.21-24 and 5.35-43, and the temple scene (11.15-19) between the incident of the fig tree (11.12-14, 20-25), expecting his audience to interpret one story with the aid of accompanying ones.

his Galilean accent: 'I do not know this man you are talking about' (14.71). After this scene the disciples disappear from the text. In this Gospel, none of them is there at the cross, or at the burial, or at the empty tomb. These last three Gospel scenes in Mark contain only women followers of Jesus, and in the end even they leave the tomb unable to carry out the request to inform the others that Jesus has risen. The Gospel's tragic closing words are: 'So they went out and fled from the tomb, for terror and amazement had seized them; and they said nothing to anyone, for they were afraid' (16.8). These words remind Mark's audience that Jesus' fate, although predicted openly several times, was not understood and not accepted by his closest followers.

Mark plainly presents a portrait of Jesus as a man of peace, who accepted the status of messiah for himself, but reinterpreted it so as to invert its military and political overtones. Mark insists, especially through his literary presentation of the disciples, that Jesus never intended to resist physically or gain control of the state by force. Perhaps his message is also that Jesus' perspective on peace is not one that people in general will readily accept—it goes against human nature.[6]

ii. *Paul*. The Book of Acts introduces Paul, before his conversion to Christianity, as a zealous Jew and a violent man. We encounter him first at Stephen's martyrdom, to which, we are told, he consented (8.1), and then extended: 'ravaging the church by entering house after house, dragging off both men and women' to prison (8.3). Before Acts recounts his conversion experience, Paul is 'still breathing threats and murder against the disciples of the Lord' (9.1). Subsequently, this violent persecutor of Christians becomes a Christian who himself is violently persecuted. Throughout Acts, and also according to Paul's

6.   The Gospels present a view of John the Baptist quite similar to Jesus. In spite of John's ability to attract large crowds and present a potential threat to Herod Antipas, ruler of Galilee, and in spite of his apparent miraculous powers (Mk 6.14), John is not said to resist arrest. Nor does he advocate taking control of the land by force. Instead, he is presented as a charismatic preacher who exhorts those who come to him to repent, and prepare for the coming end of the world and the messianic figure who will usher in the new age (Mk 1.2-8; Mt. 3.1-12; Lk. 3.1-9, 15-17). Like Jesus, John is put to death violently, and like Jesus, his power lies in playing out the role expected of him, which includes accepting violence, not inflicting it.

own letters, suffering becomes his lot. Paul graphically describes this suffering in his own defence against Christians who insisted on a closer adherence to Judaism than he thought necessary (2 Cor. 11.21-29):

> But whatever anyone dares to boast of—I am speaking as a fool—I also dare to boast of that. Are they Hebrews? So am I. Are they Israelites? So am I. Are they ministers of Christ? I am talking like a madman—I am a better one: with far greater labors, far more imprisonments, with countless floggings, and often near death. Five times I have received from the Jews the forty lashes minus one. Three times I was beaten with rods. Once I received a stoning. Three times I was shipwrecked; for a night and a day I was adrift at sea; on frequent journeys, in danger from rivers, danger from bandits, danger from my own people, danger from Gentiles, danger in the city, danger in the wilderness, danger at sea, danger from false brothers and sisters; in toil and hardship, through many a sleepless night, hungry and thirsty, often without food, cold and naked. And, besides other things, I am under daily pressure because of my anxiety for all the churches. Who is weak, and I am not weak? Who is made to stumble, and I am not indignant?

Violence certainly does not disappear from Paul's life after his conversion to Christianity. It is the source of the violence that changes.

Paul is portrayed as a staunch and zealous defender of the Christian faith, but not one who resists physically or himself inflicts physical punishment on others. He may occasionally slip away from a situation so as not to bring punishment on himself (e.g., Acts 9.23-25; 14.6), but this says less about his eagerness to flee from physical abuse than it does about the New Testament view that God, at times, desires his servants to escape life-threatening situations.

Paul in his letters also constantly encourages Christians to imitate him (e.g., Gal. 4.12; Phil. 4.17; 1 Thess. 1.6). He considers himself a role model for Christians, as the author of Acts reinforces.[7] Suffering is extolled as the ideal to be imitated. This ideal is particularly important, since Paul's letters and Acts make up more than half the New Testament. Paul's violent beginnings before his conversion effectively set off the non-violent stance of the Christian model.

To be sure, not all Christians in his day would have accepted this pacifist position. Indeed, the New Testament's stress on non-violence itself suggests that such a message needed to be reinforced within the

---

7. See, for example, Acts 23.2-5, where Paul rebukes the High Priest for wanting to strike him.

Christian communities. A passage from 2 Timothy (1.11-18) raises a further interesting possibility. This letter opens with Paul in prison, claiming that he is not ashamed of being there. Yet all the Christians who are in Asia, he tells us, have abandoned him. Could the reason be Paul's willingness to let himself be arrested and suffer passively? These verses unfortunately allow us to do no more than speculate on this possibility, but Paul's firm belief in the value of his suffering is one New Testament attitude about which we can be certain.

iii. *Simon Peter*. Simon Peter, like Paul, is made to undergo a transition from using violence as a means of effecting change to rejecting it, although the contrast is less marked. In the Gospels Simon Peter does not appear averse to using physical force. The only clear reference to him doing so is in John's version of Jesus' arrest. In this scene Simon Peter is the one 'who had a sword, drew it, struck the high priest's slave, and cut off his right ear' (18.10). Not to be forgotten as well is that his name is Simon. 'Peter is a Greek nickname (given to him by Jesus, the Gospels tell us) whose closest modern equivalent is 'Rocky'. Both his nickname and his action at Jesus' arrest (according to John, at any rate) point to a character who, in modern terms, resembles a bodyguard more than a passive resister. The Acts portrayal of Simon Peter, though, presents a different picture. After the Pentecost scene (Acts 2), in which the disciples are said to be empowered by the Holy Spirit, Simon Peter continues the leadership role he had in the Gospels. He does so without inflicting physical violence directly on anyone. To be sure, not everyone survives his presence, as the story of his encounter with Ananias and Sapphira in Acts 5.1-11 shows, but Simon Peter himself is not said to strike anyone down. Rather, he is attacked and imprisoned by others, accepts his fate without resisting, and escapes imprisonment only when God intervenes on his behalf. In this regard, Simon Peter in Acts is virtually indistinguishable from Paul.

These New Testament portrayals of Jesus, Paul and Simon Peter constantly reinforce a model of non-violent Christian interaction with others—at least when it comes to the avoidance of physical violence against others. In their missionary work and their day-to-day activities, these men appear to live out the injunction to 'turn the other cheek' (Mt. 5.39). There are a few exceptions to the rule, which I will explore in the next chapter. For instance, Paul blinds the rival magician Elymas 'for a time' (Acts 13.6-12) in order to reinforce his own authority; Peter, in the Ananias and Sapphira incident (Acts 5.1-11) to which I allude above, is undoubtedly the lead actor in a violent, vengeful scene that leads to the death of two individuals; and Jesus does not hesitate to create a physical disturbance in the temple (Mk 11.15-19; Lk. 19.45-46; Mt. 21.12-17; and especially Jn 2.13-25). Nevertheless, it is fair to say that the overwhelming impression left by the narrative portrayals of the leading figures in the New Testament is of people who are willing to accept blows and beatings without inflicting them on others.

b. *The Second Generation of Christian Leaders*
The 'Pastorals' (1 and 2 Timothy and Titus), allegedly written by Paul to two of his closest associates, provide us with the best New Testament evidence for what was expected of the second generation of Christian leaders. The message in these letters concerning peace is, once again, unequivocal: Christian leaders are expected not only to be non-violent but also to avoid violence-provoking situations. According to 1 Timothy, 'a bishop must be above reproach, married only once, temperate, sensible, respectable, hospitable, an apt teacher, not a drunkard, not violent but gentle, not quarrelsome, and not a lover of money' (3.2-3). The same message is given to Titus: 'For a bishop, as God's steward, must be blameless; he must not be arrogant or quick-tempered or addicted to wine or violent or greedy for gain; but he must be hospitable, a lover of goodness, prudent, upright, devout, and self-controlled' (1.7-8). Moreover, the leaders are urged to refrain from verbal quarrels. 'Avoid stupid controversies, genealogies, dissensions, and quarrels about the law', Paul advises Titus; 'for they are unprofitable and worthless. After a first and second admonition, have nothing more to do with anyone who causes divisions' (3.9-10). And to Timothy he says: 'The Lord's servant must not be quarrelsome but kindly to everyone, an apt teacher, patient, correcting opponents with gentleness' (2 Tim. 2.24-25).

The overall New Testament image of the church leaders (we cannot speak about the reality) is without question peace-promoting. Under no circumstance are they to engage in violence. Their task, especially as set out in the Pastorals, is to build a gentle, loving, household of God.

c. *All Christians*

The New Testament model of non-violence, represented by Jesus and the other founders, and expected of the church leaders, is meant to be followed by all other Christians. Throughout the New Testament Christians are urged to suffer violence rather than inflict it, and to effect changes that reduce potential causes for aggression toward others. Non-resistance to the political powers and a willingness to die for one's beliefs are vital parts of that message.

A dominant New Testament message is that all Christians must rid themselves of violent inclinations. One may speculate on the reasons. For instance, would the small Christian communities have survived had they preached violence against their neighbours? Were they simply postponing violence, expecting the imminent end of the world and God's judgment on humankind? Or could they have been trying to apply to social relations their understanding of Jesus' message? Whatever the reasons, the pervasiveness of this message is unquestionable. 'Put away from you all bitterness and wrath and anger', pleads the author of Ephesians (4.31). For his part, the author of Hebrews insists that being a Christian means being ready to suffer, both from others (10.32-34) and from God (12.5-11), who disciplines his children in order to lead them to perfection. Non-retaliation lies at the heart of this message. 'Do not return evil for evil' we read in 1 Pet. 3.9, Rom. 12.17-21 and 1 Thess. 5.15. To suffer rather than to retaliate or inflict suffering on others is the Christian's lot, 1 Peter emphasizes (1.6; 2.20; 3.14; 4.1, 12, 14), and 1 John insists that a Christian ought to avoid disputes with others—not because judgment awaits those who do not (which would be coercive), but in reciprocation of God's love (4.19; also 2.9; 3.11, 23; 4.20-21). This range of texts highlights their shared non-violent perspective.

The image of the disciple as child perhaps best raises this model, and Matthew's Gospel emphasizes this image most dramatically. Matthew often refers to Christians as children, or 'little ones'. He has probably inherited this usage from Mark,[8] but he elaborates on it.

---

8. I am following the scholarly consensus that Matthew and Luke, writing independently of one another, had access to copies of Mark and another written source (no longer extant but, in its reconstructed form, now called 'Q'). For the text of this source and an introduction to Q's contents, see John Kloppenborg *et al.*, *A Q/Thomas Reader* (Sonoma, CA: Polebridge Press, 1990).

Mt. 18.1-14, which is an adaptation of Mk 9.33-50, best exemplifies
this process of theological expansion. Mark's version begins as follows:

> Then they came to Capernaum; and when he was in the house he asked
> them, 'What were you arguing about on the way?' But they were silent,
> for on the way they had argued with one another who was the greatest.
> He sat down, called the twelve, and said to them, 'Whoever wants to be
> first must be last of all and servant of all.' Then he took a little child and
> put it among them; and taking it in his arms, he said to them, 'Whoever
> welcomes one such child in my name welcomes me, and whoever wel-
> comes me welcomes not me but the one who sent me.'

The Markan stress is on the need for Christians to receive children
openly, implying that a child is a valid symbol for a true disciple.
Matthew's version goes even further:

> At that time the disciples came to Jesus and asked, 'Who is the greatest in
> the kingdom of heaven?' He called a child, whom he put among them,
> and said, 'Truly I tell you, unless you change and become like children,
> you will never enter the kingdom of heaven. Whoever becomes humble
> like this child is the greatest in the kingdom of heaven. Whoever wel-
> comes one such child in my name welcomes me.'

This text makes explicit what was implicit in the Markan story:
Christians are to 'turn and become like children'. Called by Jesus
(18.2), the child stands for a disciple (or a Christian—the terms are
synonymous for Matthew). The hugging scene is left out, as one
would expect, since the child already represents a disciple. Children
are naturally Christlike, Matthew emphasizes, and adults must strive
to be childlike in order to fulfil Jesus' expectations of them. Matthew
maintains the focus on children in his narrative by omitting two
Markan incidents which have nothing to do with children (Mk 9.38-
41, 49-50), and adding a story of his own (Mt. 18.10-14):

> 'Take care that you do not despise one of these little ones; for, I tell you,
> in heaven their angels continually see the face of my Father in heaven.
> What do you think? If a shepherd has a hundred sheep, and one of them
> has gone astray, does he not leave the ninety-nine on the mountains and
> go in search of the one that went astray? And if he finds it, truly I tell you,
> he rejoices over it more than over the ninety-nine that never went astray.
> So it is not the will of your Father in heaven that one of these little ones
> should be lost.'

What does 'childlike' imply for Matthew?[9] The context suggests that humility is one characteristic: 'Whoever becomes humble like this child is the greatest in the kingdom of heaven' (18.4). This verse recalls the third beatitude, part of a collection of 'blessed' statements which inaugurate Jesus' first major sermon in this Gospel: 'Blessed are the meek, for they will inherit the earth' (5.5). In addition, the remainder of Matthew 18 (especially 18.21-35) adds the element of forgiveness and compassion, which again brings to mind the beatitudes—this time the fifth ('Blessed are the merciful') and the seventh ('Blessed are the peacemakers'). In this context, the closing words of Matthew 10 (10.38-42), a chapter concerned with discipleship which ends with a message about 'little ones', remind us of the last beatitude (5.11-12): 'Blessed are you when people revile you and persecute you and utter all kinds of evil against you falsely on my account.'

> And whoever does not take up the cross and follow me is not worthy of me. Those who find their life will lose it, and those who lose their life for my sake will find it. Whoever welcomes you welcomes me, and whoever welcomes me welcomes the one who sent me. Whoever welcomes a prophet in the name of a prophet will receive a prophet's reward; and whoever welcomes a righteous person in the name of a righteous person will receive the reward of the righteous; and whoever gives even a cup of cold water to one of these little ones in the name of a disciple—truly I tell you, none of these will lose their reward.

A true Christian, according to Matthew, is one who is able to become childlike. This transformation incorporates the qualities of humility and forgiveness, and implies a certain degree of helplessness. These transformed Christians are the ones considered blessed by Jesus in the beatitudes, and they represent for Matthew those who will soon experience God's presence fully (who enter his 'kingdom').

The New Testament texts emphasize that such a transformation does not involve resisting the political authorities. Paul, in Rom. 13.1-7, most clearly admonishes Christians to respect the legal powers of the authorities:

> Let every person be subject to the governing authorities; for there is no authority except from God, and those authorities that exist have been

---

9.   This question is different than asking what 'childlike' means to us, and also whether Matthew has a correct view of children. For instance, the 'humility', 'forgiveness' and 'compassion' stressed by Matthew's Jesus are not always reflected in parents' experience of their children!

instituted by God. Therefore whoever resists authority resists what God has appointed, and those who resist will incur judgment. For rulers are not a terror to good conduct, but to bad. Do you wish to have no fear of authority? Then do what is good, and you will receive its approval; for it is God's servant for your good. But if you do what is wrong, you should be afraid, for the authority does not bear the sword in vain! It is the servant of God to execute wrath on the wrongdoer. Therefore one must be subject, not only because of wrath but also because of conscience. For the same reason you also pay taxes, for the authorities are God's servants, busy with this very thing. Pay to all what is due them—taxes to whom taxes are due, revenue to whom revenue is due, respect to whom respect is due, honor to whom honor is due.

Violent human resistance to the political authorities is not condoned explicitly here, or for that matter anywhere else in the New Testament.

Changing lenses in the next chapter, I will argue that 'peace' that does not allow for resistance against physical oppression can be considered 'violence', especially when it is combined with a disregard for the need to transform society. 'Keeping the status quo' is arguably a violent stance since it does little to reduce the social and financial inequalities that so often lie at the root of violent outbreaks. What I would like to emphasize here is this: the New Testament insistence that political authorities be respected is accompanied at times by concern for internal transformation and social justice. This combination (how it was realized by early Christians can no longer be determined) makes the message fundamentally peace-promoting on several levels.

Hebrews 13 and 1 John 3 effectively argue for increased social awareness on the part of Christians, but the letter of James perhaps does it best (e.g., 1.26-27; 2.14-26; 3.9-18). James 2.14-17 insists:

What good is it, my brothers and sisters, if you say you have faith but do not have works? Can faith save you? If a brother or sister is naked and lacks daily food, and one of you says to them, 'Go in peace; keep warm and eat your fill,' and yet you do not supply their bodily needs, what is the good of that? So faith by itself, if it has no works, is dead.

This passage indicates that 'peace' for some Christians was thought to be possible without social justice. James, however, counters this assumption. He argues not only for peaceful coexistence in his communities but for a peace based on social justice. In this regard, his message has a modern ring to it. So too does his belief (see 1.12-15) that people should not blame God, Satan or whomever for their passionate and violent outbursts; rather, they should struggle to transform themselves in order to eliminate violent inclinations. Lasting peace, James insists, comes about through attending to the causes of violent outbursts, both within ourselves and in the ways in which we have organized our social activities.

New Testament exhortations to non-violence climax paradoxically in the glorification of martyrdom. Christians are encouraged not only to endure persecutions, but to endure them to the point of death. Eternal life is said to await those Christians who are persecuted and who die for their faith, not usually those who die in battle. Putting it in New Testament terms, the 'battle' to be fought by Christians is spiritual in nature. John and Jesus died as martyrs, Peter and Paul were willing to die,[10] and all Christians ought to imitate this model. Making martyrdom an ideal in this manner certainly is one of the strongest encouragements for non-resistance to violence.

This martyrdom model emerges not only through the actions of individuals, but also in specific exhortations, as Mark expresses in 8.34-36:

> He called the crowd with his disciples, and said to them, 'If any want to become my followers, let them deny themselves and take up their cross and follow me. For those who want to save their life will lose it, and those who lose their life for my sake, and for the sake of the gospel, will save it. For what will it profit them to gain the whole world and forfeit their life?'

Rev. 20.4-6 (see also 12.11) highlights martyrdom by insisting that Christians who die as martyrs to the faith will receive the special reward of being the only ones to live with Jesus for the thousand years that are to close the end of this age and precede the age to come:

> Then I saw thrones, and those seated on them were given authority to judge. I also saw the souls of those who had been beheaded for their testimony to Jesus and for the word of God. They had not worshipped the beast or its image and had not received its mark on their foreheads or their hands. They came to life and reigned with Christ a thousand years. (The rest of the dead did not come to life until the thousand years were ended.) This is the first resurrection. Blessed and holy are those who share in the first resurrection. Over these the second death has no power, but they will be priests of God and of Christ, and they will reign with him a thousand years.

---

10. Scholars have long puzzled over why the author of Acts does not recount the deaths of Peter and Paul. Traditions of their martyrdoms in Rome existed in the second century.

Once again, what needs to be stressed is the importance placed on accepting violence, even to the point of death. The above citation adds to this ubiquitous New Testament understanding the importance of welcoming violence. No glory comes from taking the offensive or inflicting violence; just the opposite is the case.

d. *Summary*

The history of the early Christian communities depicted in Acts, which includes all the major points listed above, effectively serves to summarize the general New Testament attitude toward peace. The ideal—probably idealized—bourgeoning Christian community in Acts is depicted as remarkably non-violent and egalitarian (2.42-47):

> They devoted themselves to the apostles' teaching and fellowship, to the breaking of bread and the prayers. Awe came upon everyone, because many wonders and signs were being done by the apostles. All who believed were together and had all things in common; they would sell their possessions and goods and distribute the proceeds to all, as any had need. Day by day, as they spent much time together in the temple, they broke bread at home and ate their food with glad and generous hearts, praising God and having the goodwill of all the people.

The interrogations and arrests of Christians, which at first do not evince a great deal of physical violence, soon begin to involve considerable Christian suffering. One example occurs in ch. 5, when the Jewish leaders, distressed at the mounting popularity of the Christian movement, summon the apostles and have them flogged (5.40-42):

> Then they ordered them not to speak in the name of Jesus, and let them go. As they left the council, they rejoiced that they were considered worthy to suffer dishonor for the sake of the name. And every day in the temple and at home they did not cease to teach and proclaim Jesus as the Messiah.

Paul's conversion, significant enough in Acts to be recounted three times (9.1-19; 22.3-21; 26.9-18), puts this message of suffering on Jesus' lips. Go to Paul, Jesus tells Ananias, 'for he is an instrument whom I have chosen to bring my name before Gentiles and kings and before the people of Israel; I myself will show him how much he must suffer for the sake of my name' (9.15-16). Paul indeed suffers throughout Acts. So do most other Christians. Although neither Paul nor Peter is said to suffer to the point of death, other Christians' martyrdoms are recounted and glorified. John's brother, James, is killed by Herod (12.2), while Stephen's death at the hands of some Jews is recounted at length in 6.8-8.1. As in the rest of the New Testament, then, non-violence in the face of violence is the Christian model set forth in Acts. This expected ideal behaviour brings to mind Gandhi more than any other public figure of our century.

3. *The Sermon on the Mount*

Many people today (not only Christians) would claim that Matthew's Sermon on the Mount (Mt. 5–7) offers a summary of Jesus' ethical demands, and that it contains some of the loftiest moral ideals ever expressed. Tolstoy and Gandhi, for instance, felt some attraction to Christianity because of these three chapters in the New Testament. A delightful Zen Buddhist story, based on a few verses from this sermon, reinforces the point.[11]

> A university student while visiting Gasan asked him: 'Have you ever read the Christian Bible?' 'No, read it to me,' said Gasan. The student opened the Bible and read from St. Matthew: 'And why take ye thought for raiment? Consider the lilies of the field, how they grow. They toil not, neither do they spin, and yet I say unto you that even Solomon in all his glory was not arrayed like one of these… Take therefore no thought for the morrow, for the morrow shall take thought for the things of itself.' Gasan said: 'Whoever uttered those words I consider an enlightened man.' The student continued reading: 'Ask and it shall be given to you, seek and ye shall find, knock and it shall be opened unto you. For everyone that asketh receiveth, and he that seeketh findeth, and to him that knocketh, it shall be opened.' Gasan remarked: 'That is excellent. Whoever said that is not far from Buddhahood.'

Within Matthew's Gospel itself the Sermon on the Mount plays an important narrative role. It is Jesus' first major proclamation,[12] and much of what follows turns out to be an expansion of the thoughts

11. From *Zen Flesh, Zen Bones*, compiled by Paul Reps (Rutland, VT: Charles E. Tuttle Co., 1957), p. 36.

12. Matthew 5–7 almost certainly is not a verbatim reproduction of a lengthy sermon that Jesus once gave. Too many specific factors speak against this possibility. One, for instance, is that much of the same material is scattered throughout the other Gospels (which version, if any, is one to accept as authentic?). Another is that the ancient practice of recounting speeches aimed at getting across the overall mood and intent, not a word-for-word reproduction, and entailed a great deal of free adaptation.

presented in these three chapters. Scholars tend to perceive this Gospel's narrative structure in one of two ways; each highlights the importance of chs. 5–7.[13] One popular breakdown treats 1.1–4.1 as the opening section which introduces Jesus, 4.17–16.20 as the 'proclamation section', and 16.21–28.20 as Jesus' journey into suffering, death and afterlife. This structure turns the Sermon on the Mount into the opening chords of the proclamation. The other common literary breakdown shows more sensitivity to the comparison the author makes between Moses and Jesus. Only in Matthew does Jesus' infancy resemble that of Moses (both escape the death inflicted on all other infants in their homeland, both are connected with Egypt); only in Matthew is Jesus' first proclamation delivered from a mountain, as was Moses' presentation of the ten commandments; and perhaps also only in Matthew can Jesus' major proclamations be broken down into five 'books', reminiscent of the first five biblical books long attributed to Moses. The bulk of Matthew's Gospel can be made to fit into five sections, each comprising narrative and discourse subsections and ending with virtually the same phrase: 'when Jesus had finished these sayings' (7.28; 11.1; 13.53; 19.1; 26.1). If this is the structure that Matthew indeed had in mind, the Sermon on the Mount takes on all that much more importance, especially given its delivery from the mountain top. In any case, however one understands Matthew's literary structure, the important point is that these three chapters form a crucial section in the opening book of the New Testament. Also not to be forgotten is that this Gospel became Christianity's most popular depiction of Jesus' life and teachings.

Matthew 5–7 emphasizes the necessity of acting properly to attain eternal life. Faith in Jesus as God's resurrected son does not suffice; rather, faith needs to be supplemented by 'good works'. In ch. 7 this point is expressed in the context of the discussion about the 'two ways' open to Christians: taking the difficult, 'narrow path' symbolizes hearing and carrying out Jesus' demands, while taking the 'wide path' entails the easier but unfruitful option of only hearing them. Matthew's Jesus makes his position unequivocal in 5.17-19:

13. An example of the first is Jack Dean Kingsbury, *Matthew as Story* (Philadelphia, PA: Fortress Press, 2nd edn, 1988 [1986]); the second structural breakdown was popularized by B.W. Bacon's *Studies in Matthew* (New York, NY: H. Hold and Co., 1930).

> Do not think that I have come to abolish the law or the prophets; I have
> come not to abolish but to fulfil. For truly I tell you, until heaven and
> earth pass away, not one letter, not one stroke of a letter, will pass from
> the law until all is accomplished. Therefore, whoever breaks one of the
> least of these commandments, and teaches others to do the same, will be
> called least in the kingdom of heaven; but whoever does them and teaches
> them will be called great in the kingdom of heaven.

The connection between proper actions and salvation is stressed
elsewhere in the New Testament (e.g., Jas 2.14-17), but receives less
attention in the Pauline corpus. In emphasizing the right for non-Jews
to become Christians without first converting to Judaism, Paul consistently downplays the importance of following Jewish 'works', by
which he means principally ritual measures such as circumcision,
dietary practices and keeping certain days holy. His many disputes
with other Christians over this issue only served to reinforce Paul's
claim in his letters that 'salvation is by faith alone'. It needs to be
stressed, though, that Paul, perhaps as much as Matthew, also believed
that the most stringent ethical demands were placed on people who
became Christians. The Sermon on the Mount, then, while stressing
proper actions to a degree rarely seen elsewhere in the New Testament,
remains consistent with the other books of the New Testament corpus.

'Acting properly' for Matthew, as 5.17-19 above indicates, means
following the demands of the biblical 'law and the prophets'; it also
means following the additional requirements presented by Jesus.
Matthew's Jesus proceeds to say, in 5.20: 'For I tell you, unless your
righteousness exceeds that of the scribes and Pharisees, you will never
enter the kingdom of heaven.' If upheld, one could argue that these
extra demands would lead a Christian directly to a non-violent
lifestyle. They are best appreciated by the six 'antitheses' which follow
in 5.21-48. These make the Mosaic law more stringent (they do not
seek to overturn it—hence, the traditional term 'antitheses' is somewhat misleading). They also encourage the disciples to maintain and
re-establish exemplary relationships with others.

The antitheses all bear directly on the issue of peace and violence.
The first is as follows:

> You have heard that it was said to those of ancient times, 'You shall not
> murder'; and 'whoever murders shall be liable to judgment.' But I say to
> you that if you are angry with a brother or sister, you will be liable to
> judgment; and if you insult a brother or sister, you will be liable to the
> council; and if you say, 'You fool,' you will be liable to the hell of fire.

> So when you are offering your gift at the altar, if you remember that your
> brother or sister has something against you, leave your gift there before
> the altar and go; first be reconciled to your brother or sister, and then
> come and offer your gift. Come to terms quickly with your accuser while
> you are on the way to court with him, or your accuser may hand you over
> to the judge, and the judge to the guard, and you will be thrown into
> prison. Truly I tell you, you will never get out until you have paid the last
> penny.

Jesus here makes anger and its related offences just as grave an
offence among Christians as murder is to the outside world. According
to this perspective, extreme violence entails not only killing people,
but also mistreating them verbally or emotionally. This is considered
so serious an offence that, when it occurs, brotherly and sisterly reconciliation is to take precedence even over the worship of God. If it does
not, a Christian cannot hope to be reconciled to God.

The second antithesis concerns lust:

> You have heard that it was said, 'You shall not commit adultery.' But I
> say to you that everyone who looks at a woman with lust has already
> committed adultery with her in his heart. If your right eye causes you to
> sin, tear it out and throw it away; it is better for you to lose one of your
> members than for your whole body to be thrown into hell. And if your
> right hand causes you to sin, cut it off and throw it away; it is better for
> you to lose one of your members than for your whole body to go into hell.

Here again, violence is said to be more than an overt, physical act. A
man (the perspective is male) has essentially already committed
adultery with a woman or raped her when he has wished it in his mind.

The third antithesis concerns divorce and compassion:

> It was also said, 'Whoever divorces his wife, let him give her a certificate
> of divorce.' But I say to you that anyone who divorces his wife, except
> on the ground of unchastity, causes her to commit adultery; and whoever
> marries a divorced woman commits adultery.

This teaching reinforces the need for Christians to consider seriously
another person's well-being. The Matthean prohibition against divorce
is based on the following logical links: marriage is for life, and
anyone remarrying actually commits adultery; a woman will almost
certainly have to be married to survive in her society; if her husband
divorces her, she will marry another and that relationship will make
both her and her new husband adulterers, since in God's eyes she
remains married to the first man; hence, a husband has a duty to his

wife not to force her into an adulterous situation—if she chooses that path herself, he is no longer responsible and may divorce her.

To this teaching the fourth antithesis adds the point that Christians cannot ignore their responsibilities. They must take full responsibility for what they say or do:

> Again, you have heard that it was said to those of ancient times, 'You shall not swear falsely, but carry out the vows you have made to the Lord.' But I say to you, Do not swear at all, either by heaven, for it is the throne of God, or by the earth, for it is his footstool, or by Jerusalem, for it is the city of the great King. And do not swear by your head, for you cannot make one hair white or black. Let your word be 'Yes, Yes' or 'No, No'; anything more than this comes from the evil one.

In all four of these antitheses Christians are expected to re-establish and maintain relationships that consider others equal.[14]

The last two antitheses explicitly reinforce the principles of non-violence underlined in the first four. The fifth one is as follows:

> You have heard that it was said, 'An eye for an eye and a tooth for a tooth.' But I say to you, Do not resist an evildoer. But if anyone strikes you on the right cheek, turn the other also; and if anyone wants to sue you and take your coat, give your cloak as well; and if anyone forces you to go one mile, go also the second mile. Give to everyone who begs from you, and do not refuse anyone who wants to borrow from you.

This injunction, it needs to be said, is not a critique of the 'eye for an eye and a tooth for a tooth' position, any more than the second antithesis criticizes the injunction against murder. The *lex talionis* (punishment in kind) worked for justice (demanding that wrongdoers be punished) and against vindictiveness (demanding that the punishment not exceed the crime). What Matthew's Jesus demands is that Christians go even beyond this sound principle of justice. They are not to seek revenge on those who have done them wrong; moreover, their non-resistance should involve actively improving the relationship between people.[15] The last antithesis (5.43-48) encourages an *imitatio*

14. Daniel Patte emphasizes this point eloquently in *The Gospel according to Matthew: A Structural Commentary on Matthew's Faith* (Philadelphia, PA: Fortress Press, 1987), pp. 60-108.

15. Luke's version of this teaching (6.29-30) is different in detail but identical in intent: 'If anyone strikes you on the cheek, offer the other also; and from anyone who takes away your coat do not withhold even your shirt. Give to everyone who begs from you; and if anyone takes away your goods, do not ask for them again.'

Dei, in the sense that people should strive to fulfil their potential:

> You have heard that it was said, 'You shall love your neighbour and hate
> your enemy.' But I say to you, Love your enemies and pray for those
> who persecute you, so that you may be children of your Father in heaven;
> for he makes his sun rise on the evil and on the good, and sends rain on
> the righteous and on the unrighteous. For if you love those who love you,
> what reward do you have? Do not even the tax collectors do the same?
> And if you greet only your brothers and sisters, what more are you doing
> than others? Do not even the Gentiles do the same? Be perfect, therefore,
> as your heavenly Father is perfect.[16]

The stress here is on non-violence as an inner disposition that is applicable to all people, regardless of who they are or what relationship they have to one another.

The message found in these antitheses, if carried out, would make it virtually impossible for Christians to support war or to participate in most forms of violence, however broadly defined. This cannot be said strongly enough. Physical violence is clearly prohibited, and other forms are minimized given the inner transformations and the kinds of human relationships that are expected. Other aspects of the Sermon on

---

The 'coat and cloak' part of the teaching is set in a different context. Luke's Jesus has robbery in mind, so he says: if a robber comes to you and grabs the (outer) cloak off your back, give that person your (inner) coat as well. We might now say: if a robber grabs your coat, also give him/her the shirt off your back. Matthew's Jesus has a courtroom in mind: if you are brought to court and sued, and the judge forces you to give up your coat, go further and give to your accuser your cloak as well (according to Jewish law, a person's outer garment could not be taken away permanently). Matthew's intensification (give up more than you are legally required to) and Luke's (give the robber more than is taken) both make the point that the Christian who suffers violence is encouraged to take the initiative to suffer even more (at least in the short term, for such a practice would also tend to reduce further abuse). Another Zen story makes a similar point (*Zen Flesh, Zen Bones*, p. 27):

> Ryokan, a Zen master, lived the simplest kind of life in a little hut at the foot of a
> mountain. One evening a thief visited the hut only to discover there was nothing in it
> to steal. Ryokan returned and caught him. 'You may have come a long way to visit
> me', he told the prowler, 'and you should not return empty-handed. Please take my
> clothes as a gift.' The thief was bewildered. He took the clothes and slunk away.
> Ryokan sat naked, watching the moon. 'Poor fellow', he mused, 'I wish I could give
> him this beautiful moon.'

16. Luke's parallel passage (6.36) reads, in closing: 'Be merciful, just as your Father is merciful.'

the Mount enforce these points. The beatitudes (5.3-12), which strike the opening chords, are one example:

> Blessed are the meek... the merciful... the peacemakers... those who are persecuted... Blessed are you when people revile you and persecute you and utter all kinds of evil against you falsely on my account. Rejoice and be glad, for your reward is great in heaven, for in the same way they persecuted the prophets who were before you.

The 'golden rule' of 7.12 is another: 'In everything do to others as you would have them do to you.' In short, Matthew's Sermon on the Mount presents an eloquent plea for non-violent behaviour coupled with a willingness to accept suffering at the hands of others.

4. *The Parables*

A parable is a short story depicting an everyday situation, which functions to tease its audience into reflecting on their thoughts and behaviour.[17] Parables tend to destabilize the hearer by not providing a direct answer to a specific question, and by implying that reality is not fully as one sees or experiences it. One example is Jesus' Parable of the Sower as represented in Mk 4.3-9:

> Listen! A sower went out to sow. And as he sowed, some seed fell on the path, and the birds came and ate it up. Other seed fell on rocky ground, where it did not have much soil, and it sprang up quickly, since it had no depth of soil. And when the sun rose, it was scorched; and since it had no root, it withered away. Other seed fell among thorns, and the thorns grew up and choked it, and it yielded no grain. Other seed fell into good soil and brought forth grain, growing up and increasing and yielding thirty and sixty and a hundredfold.' And he said, 'Let anyone with ears to hear listen!'

Typical of the parabolic form in this passage are the following points. First, the story, on the whole, is plausible; it emerges from the everyday lives of first-century Jews. For instance, sowing in Palestine was occasionally done before plowing, and some seeds ended up on the paths and rocks and amid thorns. Second, something in the story is unexpected or exaggerated. In this case, the yield ('thirty and sixty

---

17. A parable can also entice people to judge themselves without being aware of it at first. The classic example occurs in 2 Sam. 12.1-5, in which Nathan tells David a story about a rich landowner who steals a poor man's only ewe lamb. The story's captivating quality leads David to exclaim: 'That man deserves to die', to which Nathan responds: that man is like you, who seduced Uriah's wife, Bathsheba.

and a hundredfold') is out of proportion to normal experience (a very good yield was about tenfold). Finally, the point of this story is not to teach something about agriculture, but to lead people to reflect on their lives. A comparison is implied (in many other parables it is stated explicitly: 'The kingdom of God is like...'). The explanation which Mark adds shortly after (4.13-20), while not exhausting the meaning of this parable,[18] indicates how parables could be understood by early Christians:

> And he said to them, 'Do you not understand this parable? Then how will you understand all the parables? The sower sows the word. These are the ones on the path where the word is sown: when they hear, Satan immediately comes and takes away the word that is sown in them. And these are the ones sown on rocky ground: when they hear the word, they immediately receive it with joy. But they have no root, and endure only for a while; then, when trouble or persecution arises on account of the word, immediately they fall away. And others are those sown among the thorns: these are the ones who hear the word, but the cares of the world, and the lure of wealth, and the desire for other things come in and choke the word, and it yields nothing. And these are the ones sown on the good soil: they hear the word and accept it and bear fruit, thirty and sixty and a hundredfold.'

The New Testament parables are important for a variety of reasons. Among academics their interest lies mainly in what they may tell us about the historical Jesus—the man who actually lived and taught in Galilee two thousand years ago. Not every one of Jesus' parables recounted by the Gospel writers goes back directly to Jesus, to be sure, especially in their present form, but a few might.[19] That is a

18. The scholarly consensus is that the parables told by Jesus were simple stories that could be interpreted in many different ways, and that over the years the stories lost their connection with everyday life as they increasingly became allegorized. In an allegory each of the elements in the story represents something else, and the audience needs a key to unlock the hidden meaning. Paul presents an allegory in Galatians 4.21-26, and Matthew's 'parable' of the marriage feast (22.1-10) is far more allegorical than Luke's version of the story (Lk. 14.15-24). Mark allegorically interprets the Parable of the Sower in 4.13-20. Influential books on parables still include the following: C.H. Dodd, *The Parables of the Kingdom* (New York, NY: Scribner, rev. edn, 1961 [1936]); J. Jeremias, *The Parables of Jesus* (trans. S.H. Hooke; London: SCM Press, 3rd edn, 1972 [1936]); and Dan O. Via, *The Parables: Their Literary and Existential Dimension* (Philadelphia, PA: Fortress Press, 1967).

19. For a discussion of this historical issue, see *The Parables of Jesus, Red Letter Edition: A Report of the Jesus Seminar* (eds. Robert W. Funk, Bernard

promising prospect in a field that, since the turn of the century, has emphasized how very little can in fact be said about the historical Jesus.[20] The more than 40 parables attributed to Jesus in the New Testament represent the most distinctive known form of his speech. No historical figure in the ancient world has had as many parables attributed to them.

Both the parabolic form of teaching and the contents of the parables themselves are important for appreciating the New Testament focus on peace. To be sure, many parables are bizarre and even offensive to modern readers (were I wearing my other set of glasses, I might well see violence-promoting components). Still, in this chapter, and with considerable justification, I would argue that it is difficult if not impossible to take the parables seriously and continue to inflict violence on others. Let me explore this particular reading of Jesus' parables.

The parables encourage Christians to transform themselves internally and, in the process, increasingly minimize their worldly pre-occupations. In this regard, the similarity to the message of the Sermon on the Mount is striking. Some urge a childlike confidence in God. Two clear examples of such 'counter-cultural' parables occur in Luke 18.2-5 and 11.5-8:

> He said, 'In a certain city there was a judge who neither feared God nor had respect for people. In that city there was a widow who kept coming to him and saying, "Grant me justice against my opponent." For a while he refused; but later he said to himself, "Though I have no fear of God and no respect for anyone, yet because this widow keeps bothering me, I will grant her justice, so that she may not wear me out by continually coming."'
>
> And he said to them, 'Suppose one of you has a friend, and you go to him at midnight and say to him, "Friend, lend me three loaves of bread;

Brandon Scott, and James R. Butts; Sonoma, CA: Polebridge Press, 1988).

20. Some influential books on the historical Jesus include the following: Marcus Borg, *Conflict, Holiness and Politics in the Teachings of Jesus* (Queenston, NY: Edwin Mellen Press, 1984); John Dominic Crossan, *The Historical Jesus: The Life of a Mediterranean Jewish Peasant* (New York, NY: HarperSanFrancisco, 1991); Richard Horsley, *Jesus and the Spiral of Violence* (San Francisco, CA: Harper and Row, 1987); John P. Meier, *A Marginal Jew: Rethinking the Historical Jesus* (2 vols.; New York, NY: Doubleday, 1991–94); E.P. Sanders, *Jesus and Judaism* (Philadelphia, PA: Fortress Press, 1985); Morton Smith, *Jesus the Magician* (San Francisco, CA: Harper and Row, 1978); Geza Vermes, *Jesus the Jew: A Historian's Reading of the Gospels* and *The Religion of Jesus the Jew* (Philadelphia, PA: Fortress Press, 1973–93).

for a friend of mine has arrived, and I have nothing to set before him."
And he answers from within, "Do not bother me; the door has already
been locked, and my children are with me in bed; I cannot get up and give
you anything." I tell you, even though he will not get up and give him
anything because he is his friend, at least because of his persistence he
will get up and give him whatever he needs.'

Both these parables present arguments from the lesser to the greater:
if a person heeds to the other's distress (either to get rid of that
person, or as a friendly gesture), how much more will God heed to
human demands! They reinforce the point that humans are to place
their trust and confidence in God, and not attempt to control matters
through their own intervention. Accepting this teaching would
seriously undermine a willingness to solve problems violently.

Parables often focus on God. Some insist on recognition of the
divine in the world. 'The kingdom of heaven is like a merchant in
search of fine pearls; on finding one pearl of great value, he went and
sold all that he had and bought it' (Mt. 13.45-46). Others attempt to
elicit a committed response to this presence. The content of some of
the parables also reminds Christians of the implications should they
fail to respond. The Parable of the Great Supper, told in the New
Testament both by Luke (14.16-24) and by Matthew (22.1-4), sketches
the dire consequences of ignoring the special invitation now being
offered to humanity. Luke's version is as follows:

Then Jesus said to him, 'Someone gave a great dinner and invited many.
At the time for the dinner he sent his slave to say to those who had been
invited, "Come; for everything is ready now." But they all alike began to
make excuses. The first said to him, "I have bought a piece of land, and I
must go out and see it; please accept my regrets." Another said, "I have
bought five yoke of oxen, and I am going to try them out; please accept
my regrets." Another said, "I have just been married, and therefore I
cannot come." So the slave returned and reported this to his master. Then
the owner of the house became angry and said to his slave, "Go out at
once into the streets and lanes of the town and bring in the poor, the
crippled, the blind, and the lame." And the slave said, "Sir, what you
ordered has been done, and there is still room." Then the master said to
the slave, "Go out into the roads and lanes, and compel people to come in,
so that my house may be filled. For I tell you, none of those who were
invited will taste my dinner."'

An equally challenging manner of reminding people to respond occurs
in Luke 16.1-8:

Then, Jesus said to the disciples, 'There was a rich man who had a manager, and charges were brought to him that this man was squandering his property. So he summoned him and said to him, "What is this that I hear about you? Give me an accounting of your management, because you cannot be my manager any longer." Then the manager said to himself, "What will I do, now that my master is taking the position away from me? I am not strong enough to dig, and I am ashamed to beg. I have decided what to do so that, when I am dismissed as manager, people may welcome me into their homes." So, summoning his master's debtors one by one, he asked the first, "How much do you owe my master?" He answered, "A hundred jugs of olive oil." He said to him, "Take your bill, sit down quickly, and make it fifty." Then he asked another, "And how much do you owe?" He replied, "A hundred containers of wheat." He said to him, "Take your bill and make it eighty." And his master commended the dishonest manager because he had acted shrewdly; for the children of this age are more shrewd in dealing with their own generation than are the children of light.'

The manager in this parable has few redeeming qualities except his ability to survive: he recognizes the crisis facing him and responds desperately. Why in the end is he praised instead of condemned? It is because of his ability to respond in order to avert disaster. Again, this is a 'lesser to greater' type of argument: if a manager responds in such a manner, faced with his problems, all the more should Jesus' followers respond to the invitation to recognize the divine presence.

The parables, then, encourage inner transformation and a renewed appreciation of a greater-than-human presence, but in what way are Christians expected to be transformed? First, they are expected to be open to new ways of thinking and acting. One expression of this element of transformation is found in Mt. 20.1-15:

For the kingdom of heaven is like a landowner who went out early in the morning to hire laborers for his vineyard. After agreeing with the laborers for the usual daily wage, he sent them into his vineyard. When he went out about nine o'clock, he saw others standing idle in the marketplace; and he said to them, 'You also go into the vineyard, and I will pay you whatever is right.' So they went. When he went out again about noon and about three o'clock, he did the same. And about five o'clock he went out and found others standing around; and he said to them, 'Why are you standing here idle all day?' They said to him, 'Because no one has hired us.' He said to them, 'You also go into the vineyard.' When evening came, the owner of the vineyard said to his manager, 'Call the laborers and give them their pay, beginning with the last and then going to the first.' When those hired about five o'clock came, each of them received the usual daily wage. Now when the first came, they thought they would receive more; but each of them also received the usual daily wage. And when they received it, they grumbled against the landowner, saying, 'These last worked only one hour, and you have made them equal to us who have borne the burden of the day and the scorching heat.' But he replied to one of them, 'Friend, I am doing you no wrong; did you not agree with me for the usual daily wage? Take what belongs to you and go; I choose to give to this last the same as I give to you. Am I not allowed to do what I choose with what belongs to me? Or are you envious because I am generous?'

From the workers' perspective, the complaint seems quite justified, but they are being challenged to discard their preconceived ideas about who deserves what. Similarly, the Parable of the Good Samaritan (Lk. 10.30-37) challenges its audience to rethink who is 'good'. The force of this well-known parable tends to be weakened for a twentieth-century audience, which has difficulty appreciating the hatred felt by most Jews toward Samaritans in Jesus' day, compared to the respect felt toward many of the religious leaders. One need only substitute modern equivalents to appreciate the force of this parable anew.

Just then a lawyer stood up to test Jesus… He asked Jesus, 'Who is my neighbour?' Jesus replied, 'A man was going down from Jerusalem to Jericho, and fell into the hands of robbers, who stripped him, beat him, and went away, leaving him half dead. Now by chance a priest was going down that road; and when he saw him, he passed by on the other side. So likewise a Levite, when he came to the place and saw him, passed by on the other side. But a Samaritan while travelling came near him; and when he saw him, he was moved with pity. He went to him and bandaged his wounds, having poured oil and wine on them. Then he put him on his own animal, brought him to an inn, and took care of him. The next day he took out two denarii, gave them to the innkeeper, and said, 'Take care of him; and when I come back, I will repay you whatever more you spend.' Which of these three, do you think, was a neighbour to the man who fell into the hands of the robbers?' He said, 'The one who showed mercy.' Jesus said to him, 'Go and do likewise.'

The Parable of the Pharisee and the Tax Collector (Lk. 18.9-14) makes the same point: presuppositions about who is 'good' and who is not need to be reconsidered.

These parables encourage non-violent behaviour; others extol compassion as part of this transformation. The message is simple: God forgives us, so we ought to reciprocate by forgiving one another. This attitude is implied in the Parable of the Prodigal Son (Lk. 15.11-32). It is also the dominant message of Matthew 18.23-34:

> For this reason the kingdom of heaven may be compared to a king who wished to settle accounts with his slaves. When he began the reckoning, one who owed him ten thousand talents [roughly five billion dollars] was brought to him; and, as he could not pay, his lord ordered him to be sold, together with his wife and children and all his possessions, and payment to be made. So the slave fell on his knees before him, saying, 'Have patience with me, and I will pay you everything.' And out of pity for him, the lord of that slave released him and forgave him the debt. But that same slave, as he went out, came upon one of his fellow slaves who owed him a hundred denarii [roughly ten thousand dollars]; and seizing him by the throat, he said, 'Pay what you owe.' Then his fellow slave fell down and pleaded with him, 'Have patience with me, and I will pay you.' But he refused; then he went and threw him into prison until he would pay the debt. When his fellow slaves saw what had happened, they were greatly distressed, and they went and reported to their lord all that had taken place. Then his lord summoned him and said to him, 'You wicked slave! I forgave you all that debt because you pleaded with me. Should you not have had mercy on your fellow slave, as I had mercy on you?' And in anger his lord handed him over to be tortured until he would pay his entire debt.

Placing the parables in their New Testament context further supports their relevance to the issue of peace. The childlike model idealized in several of them brings to mind the broader New Testament exhortation that followers of Jesus should strive to resemble children. Matthew, in particular, linked this image with forgiveness, humility and the willingness to accept suffering even unto death. The reorientation is away from acquiring material goods toward fellowship and spiritual matters. The parables expand the understanding of what it means to be childlike by highlighting the child's ability to be open to new possibilities, not prejudging situations and people. In a broader New Testament context, then, the parabolic stress on inner transformation, especially when coupled with renewed openness to people and to life itself, is directly relevant to a broad understanding of peace. Connected to this, most importantly, is the evangelists' depiction of Jesus as transcending social boundaries by associating with prostitutes and tax collectors, and by touching lepers. The Parable of the Great Supper mentioned above encourages just such social boundary-transcending behaviour.

Many parables present unusual protagonists. The landowner who pays everyone the same wage, regardless of the hours they toiled for him (Mt. 20.1-15), is one of these. The unscrupulous manager in Lk. 16.1-8 is perhaps the most challenging. Almost certainly these characters were introduced in order to encourage people to reconsider their priorities and presuppositions, and encourage change in the general direction intended by the New Testament writers. Historians of religion recognize similarities in other religious traditions. Zen Buddhist stories, for instance, often had the same intent. Consider the following example.[21]

> Nanin, a Japanese master during the Meiji era (1868–1912), received a university professor who came to inquire about Zen. Nanin served tea. He poured his visitor's cup full and then kept pouring. The professor watched the overflow until he no longer could restrain himself. 'It is over-full. No more will go in!' 'Like this cup,' Nanin said, 'you are full of your own opinions and speculations. How can I show you Zen unless you first empty your cup?'

Jesus' parables promote forgiveness and an appreciation of the mysterious nature of our world. They challenge people to view others, regardless of their status, as equals. They teach that to act impulsively and violently is to satisfy a base need for anger and revenge that will only lead to unhappiness. They counsel that it takes reflection and inner transformation in order to counter these violent inclinations, and they tease their listeners into beginning that process of transformation. For all these reasons, parables play a vital role in the New Testament's concern for peace.

5. *The Imminent Demise of the World*

Early Christians believed that the world was about to end. Moreover, they saw themselves living not only near the very end of human history but, as a result of Jesus' death and resurrection, in a brief intermediary age that already contained some of the possibilities of the spiritual age to come. By their own assessment, they were in the world but not of it. This ambivalent situation elicited some anxiety, for included in this perception of reality was the double uncertainty of precisely when the new age would begin fully, and who would be part of the group to avoid eternal damnation when Jesus returned to destroy the world and pass judgment on humankind.

21. *Zen Flesh, Zen Bones*, p. 19.

The New Testament makes this particular end-time concern abundantly clear. The book of Revelation, for instance, is devoted almost entirely (chs. 4–22) to recounting again and again precisely what horrors are expected before the 'end' (the *eschaton*) arrives. Similarly, the Synoptic Gospels all have chapters in which Jesus is made to discuss the events leading up to this end (Mk 13; Mt. 24; Lk. 21). The author of 1 John takes the presence of 'antichrists' in his community as a sign that the coming 'day of the Lord' is imminent (1 Jn 2.18-29). The letters of Paul and 2 Peter are particularly relevant, since they reveal ways in which this concern disturbed some early Christian communities.

Paul, in both of his letters to the Thessalonians, had to face problems arising from his preaching that the end was fast approaching. He himself makes it clear (1 Thess. 1.8-10) that this topic played an important role in his initial preaching to the Thessalonians:

> For the word of the Lord has sounded forth from you not only in Macedonia and in Achaia, but in every place your faith in God has become known, so that we have no need to speak about it. For the people of those regions report about us what kind of welcome we had among you, and how you turned to God from idols, to serve a living and true God, and to wait for his Son from heaven, whom he raised from the dead—Jesus, who rescues us from the wrath that is coming.

In 1 Thessalonians we encounter Paul's community troubled by the fact that at least one of their members has died since Paul left them. This unexpected situation posed a problem. In his teachings to them concerning the end time, Paul indicated what they could expect when Jesus soon returned, but he did not indicate what would happen to anyone who died before Jesus' return. They ask for his advice and he responds (4.13-18) with words of comfort. Their anxiety helps us to appreciate how imminent an end was anticipated by these Christians. Do not worry, Paul counsels them: those who have died will not be forgotten by God; Jesus himself taught that the dead will have the advantage of rising up with him to meet God before the rest of us are allowed:

> But we do not want you to be uninformed, brothers and sisters, about those who have died, so that you may not grieve as others do who have no hope. For since we believe that Jesus died and rose again, even so, through Jesus, God will bring with him those who have died. For this we declare to you by the word of the Lord, that we who are alive, who are

left until the coming of the Lord, will by no means precede those who
have died. For the Lord himself, with a cry of command, with the
archangel's call and with the sound of God's trumpet, will descend from
heaven, and the dead in Christ will rise first. Then we who are alive, who
are left, will be caught up in the clouds together with them to meet the
Lord in the air; and so we will be with the Lord forever. Therefore
encourage one another with these words.

In 2 Thessalonians Paul faces another problem resulting from the
expectation of the end: something and someone has convinced his
community that Jesus has in fact returned and that the last days are
upon them. Paul writes to inform his community that they are mis-
taken. He reminds them of the signs for which they must look in
anticipation of the true return of Jesus (2.1-12). In both of these
letters, then, and in others as well (e.g., 1 Cor. 15.24-28; Col. 3.4),
Paul reveals that the issue of the coming end was often on his mind.

The last chapter of 2 Peter also addresses a related issue. Some
second generation Christians (the writer calls them 'scoffers') are
frustrated because the world has not ended as expected, in spite of
their leaders' continuing assurances that it would, and they are sowing
doubts in the minds of others. Second Peter quotes their words:
'Where is the promise of his coming? For ever since our ancestors
died, all things continue as they were from the beginning of creation!'
(3.4). The author attempts to counter this charge. First, he says, the
presence of such scoffers is expected 'in the last days' (3.3). More
importantly, in his view, these sceptical remarks ignore the workings
of God's mind. God has delayed the end partly because his sense of
time is different than ours ('with the Lord one day is like a thousand
years, and a thousand years are like one day'—3.8) and partly out of a
desire to give people as much time as possible to 'come to repentance'
(3.9).[22] 'But the day of the Lord will come like a thief, and then the
heavens will pass away with a loud noise, and the elements will be
dissolved with fire, and the earth and everything that is done on it will
be disclosed' (3.10). The author's closing exhortations (3.11-14)
follow logically from the above:

Since all these things are to be dissolved in this way, what sort of persons
ought you to be in leading lives of holiness and godliness, waiting for and
hastening the coming of the day of God, because of which the heavens

22. These two reasons stand in tension. The first assumes that God's sense of
time is different; the second assumes that it is the same.

will be set ablaze and dissolved, and the elements will melt with fire? But,
in accordance with his promise, we wait for new heavens and a new
earth, where righteousness is at home.

The early Christian preoccupation with the end times, or eschatology, is firmly entrenched in the New Testament and well known to
scholars. Often, though, it now gets under-appreciated and over-
looked, particularly by 'liberals', for whom this understanding of
reality is so very different from theirs. What is more, the early
Christians turned out to be wrong in their expectation of a swift end
to their world, and for some Christians that remains a difficult
proposition to accept.[23] Still, the eschatological urgency which lies
behind much of the New Testament preaching can help us to appreciate the peace message all the more. 'Living every moment as though it
were the last' also is a goal transferable to people who do not necessarily share the specific New Testament expectations about the end
times.

What would it have meant for these people to expect the end to
come any day? A modern analogy might help sharpen the question:
what would I do if I were convinced that the entire world would be
destroyed in six months (e.g., in a nuclear or environmental
catastrophe), if I believed in the existence of a God who judged individuals at death, and if I felt that my actions and beliefs during these
next six months would irrevocably determine my existence for
eternity? This scenario is roughly what the earliest Christians faced,
and the New Testament reveals that many acted as one would expect.
They persistently tried to convince others of the truth of their beliefs
in the imminent catastrophe awaiting all of humanity, and the need to
make full use of what little time was left. The New Testament letters
testify to that missionary zeal, as do the endings of Matthew and John,
and the entire book of Acts. Christians tended to show no inclination
to fight over the acquisition of land and material goods; rather, they
taught against acquiring wealth ('it is easier for a camel to go through

23. Other modern Christians are able to take quite seriously both the inspired
quality of the Scriptures and eschatology by assuming that the imminent end time
predicted in the New Testament applies not to a first-century context but to our own.
The popularity of these beliefs is quite remarkable. See especially Hal Lindsey's
The Late Great Planet Earth (with C.C. Carlson; New York, NY: Bantam Books,
1973 [1970]), which sold more paperback copies than any other non-fiction book
in the 1970s.

the eye of a needle than for someone who is rich to enter the kingdom
of God'—Mt. 19.24) and in favour of sharing all property (Acts
4.32–5.11). They did not resist the political and religious authorities
(Rom. 13.1-7). They abandoned their jobs (as a result, Paul occasionally
must encourage his communities to keep working; e.g., 2 Thess. 3.6-
13). They attempted to lead perfect lives (Matthew's Sermon on the
Mount). They debated the usefulness of marriage and sex (Paul, for
example, in 1 Cor. 7 encourages celibacy for those who can control
their sexual urges). And as the years went by some of them gave
up hope. The author of Hebrews, one easily discerns, tries various
psychological tactics to keep his members from giving up faith in the
imminent end—telling them, for example (6.4), that if they abandon
their faith they cannot convert again.

The implications for peace are obvious. The New Testament documents were aimed at Christian communities for whom violence inten-
tionally inflicted on others was seen as damning, and for whom the
major sources of violence (greed, revenge, insensitivity to others, lack
of purpose in life) were reduced and at times even removed by this
sense of living in the end times. The eschatological orientation
certainly helps to explain at least in part why the New Testament
demands for peaceful and non-violent behaviour are so radical and
categorical. To live every moment as though it were the last is also a
perspective whose implications can be appreciated by both secular and
non-secular folk.

6. *Paul's Ethic of Peace*

The belief in the imminent end lies behind two Pauline views which
go a long way toward qualifying him as an 'apostle of peace': his ideal
of equality and his spirit of compromise. Paul's belief in the imminent
demise of the world—the 'old age'—contributed to his willingness
occasionally to compromise his principles. What mattered to him
especially was keeping the members of his communities at peace with
one another and with the outside world, allowing them to concentrate
on the momentous event they all expected would soon take place. Paul
also believed that the power of the divine presence worked so strongly
within him that he was already able to experience some of the realities
of the age to come, an age that would include full equality for all of
God's children. His letters reveal that he passed these beliefs on to his

followers as ideals to be presently touched and more fully realized in the near future.

Both these views must be qualified. Paul's projection of equality between slaves and their masters, men and women, and Jews and non-Jews, however committed he may have been, remained an ideal that he often considered unnecessary to implement. With the end fast approaching, as he believed, he was not interested in effecting what we might call 'real changes' in the social, legal, and political structures. Moreover, Paul's spirit of compromise did not lead to complete democracy in his communities. Frequently, when someone questioned his authority to lead, or his foundational claim that non-Jews did not have to convert to Judaism to join his communities, Paul's response was unequivocal: he was in control and his view was correct. These limitations, however, need not make us overlook Paul's peace-promoting side. To argue for equality and to respect other people's opinions, as he often does in his letters, is to tread the road to peace.

Paul's ideal of equality is expressed most succinctly in Gal. 3.26-28:

> In Christ you are all children of God through faith. As many of you as were baptized into Christ have clothed yourself with Christ. There is no longer Jew or Greek, there is no longer slave or free, there is no longer male and female; for all of you are one in Christ Jesus.

The context is initiatory: Paul reminds the Galatians that when they were baptized and joined the community they stripped themselves not only of their clothes but of their old selves, emerging from the water prepared to be clothed anew in Christ and to join a group where all distinctions were meaningless in the eyes of God: 'for all of you are one in Christ Jesus'. God is no longer thought to show a preference for free, male Jews. This emphasis on equality and its link to baptism recurs in 1 Cor. 12.12-13 and Col. 3.9-11 (although both explicitly exclude the component of sexual equality).[24] These references, taken together, strongly suggest that at the heart of the Pauline Christians'

---

24. A close examination of the last phrase in Gal. 3.28 reveals a difference which might be important. The first two phrases are worded similarly: 'There is no longer Jew or Greek, there is no longer slave or free.' But the third reads, 'there is no longer male and female'. This could be a different way of saying the same thing, i.e., breaking down the biological distinctions; however, treating 'male and female' as a unit, and equating it with 'marriage and family', for instance (as it so often was in Jewish literature), might indicate that it referred to abolishing the tradition of marriage and family (thereby allowing men and women to gain their status otherwise).

conversion experience was the acknowledgment that all Christians are equal, and the belief that this equality would fully become reality as soon as Jesus returned to usher in the new age. This is what Christians heard when they participated in the baptisms of new members and this is what they continued to hear from Paul. It was not a common message in the ancient Greco-Roman and Jewish worlds. At the heart of the Christian experience in the Pauline communities, then, lay the seed for peace, since lasting peace, one can argue, cannot prevail without recognition of equality.

In spite of his insistence on equality, Paul is sometimes criticized now by those who are intent on 'democratizing' their churches. The criticism comes partly because our concerns are not always his. His letters address issues that were important to him and his communities. They reflect considerable struggle over whether people converting to Christianity were becoming Jews and were therefore required to pass through Jewish initiation rites (circumcision for males, the presentation of a temple offering and perhaps also baptism for all), or whether they were converting to a form of religiosity that grew out of Judaism but had become a separate entity. Paul was one of a growing number of Christians who believed strongly in the latter, and his letters attest to this preoccupation. They also attest to the many confrontations he had with other Christians who disagreed with him on this point. That 'there is no longer Jew or Greek' in the eyes of God mattered tremendously to Paul. It matters little to us now (and in fact stopped mattering much to Christians even in the second century), because most people take it for granted that a person's birth or race does not dictate his/her possible relationship with God. What mattered to us only a century ago was the issue of slavery, and what matters to us now is the issue of sexual equality. On both of these issues Paul does not go as far as many would like. He has the opportunity to speak clearly against the institution of slavery in the letter to Philemon, which is directly concerned with the plight of the runaway slave Onesimus. He has numerous opportunities to treat women as full and equal partners...but on both of these issues he hesitates and, many would argue, does not go far enough. In spite of the sensitivity he shows to Onesimus' plight, and in spite of the many women he recognizes as co-workers in his letters,[25] slaves in Paul's letters remain

25. For a fine summary of Paul's openness to women see Peter Richardson's *Paul's Ethic of Freedom* (Philadelphia, PA: Westminster Press, 1970) and 'From

subservient to their masters and women to their husbands.[26]

Does this ambivalent position invalidate Paul's peace-promoting ideal? Since we are now examining this material through a 'peace lens', so to speak, let us give Paul the benefit of the doubt for the moment. His unwillingness to carry through fully with his ideal is understandable given his expectation that the world would soon end. In his eyes it would have been useless to work toward significant societal changes given the transitory nature of the present world, and senseless to risk the destruction of his communities over this issue. Had the Roman authorities heard of a group advocating freedom to all slaves, they certainly would have arrested all of its members. Paul probably also would not have risked the chance of his communities breaking apart from within over these issues. Given his frame of mind and the period in which he wrote, his refusal to push for full equality on all levels is understandable. The more idealistic position would have had disastrous consequences. His ideal itself, though, still stands out, and the New Testament has captured it as though in amber. Christendom's refusal to make it a reality once the first-century situation changed perhaps says more about Paul's successors than about Paul himself.

Paul's practice of accommodation is equally peace-promoting. He frequently shows a willingness to take other people's views into account and allow for the existence of diversity in his communities. One example, found in Romans, is his attempt to convince the predominantly non-Jewish component of that Christian community to treat Jewish Christians as equals (ch. 14), and still consider the non-Christian Jews as God's chosen ones (chs. 9–11). Both Jewish and non-Jewish Christians, he argues, are members of the same family, in spite of their differences; and both Christians and Jews are part of God's overall plan, in spite of the present rejection of the Christian message by most Jews.

First Corinthians provides the most concrete examples of this 'ethic of accommodation'.[27] This letter is particularly revealing because it is

Apostles to Virgins', *Toronto Journal of Theology* 2 (1986), pp. 232-61.

26. For instance, 1 Cor. 11.2-6 indicates that Paul believed in a hierarchical understanding of reality with God on top, Jesus next in line, men below that, and women at the bottom.

27. For a more thorough discussion of what follows, see John Coolidge Hurd, Jr,

partly a series of direct responses to specific questions from the Corinthian church. Some of the letter's background can be reconstructed from the evidence provided by Paul himself: he visited Corinth and founded a community (2.1); after his departure he wrote them a letter, which is now lost (5.9); the Corinthians continued the conversation by responding (7.1); and Paul answered from Ephesus (16.8). His response, both to their specific questions (especially in chs. 7–16) and to what he has heard about the community (especially in chs. 1–6), is now called '1 Corinthians'. His answers to three of their questions—concerning sexual intercourse (ch. 7), dietary practices (chs. 8–10), and speaking in tongues (chs. 12–14)—help us to appreciate his ethical stance.

The Corinthian question to Paul in ch. 7 appears to be: is it really appropriate for a man 'to touch a woman' (7.1)? Paul's response shows sensitivity both for the value of the Corinthian claim (that it is likely not appropriate) and for the legitimate counter claims of others. He answers in the following manner. In theory, you are correct. For 'the appointed time has grown short' (7.29) and a Christian while awaiting the end can better concentrate on spiritual matters by avoiding sexual contact. 'I wish that all were as I myself am' (7.7), able presently to avoid sexual encounters. I encourage others to act likewise. But in practice not everyone can, so do what is best for you. This will usually entail remaining married (7.17-31). Paul concludes by counselling that, in his opinion, they are better off abstaining from sex (if married) or not marrying at all, but he leaves it to the Corinthians themselves to decide. He recognizes that there can be legitimate differences of opinion. He gives his opinion, supports it, but does not seek to coerce them directly into acting against their will.

Chapters 8–10 address an issue that must be understood in its historical context. Much of the food—and almost all of the (more valuable) meat—sold in the first century was first offered in thanks to one of the gods. Very little, if any, was actually burnt as an offering or laid in front of a statue, but all of it was thought to belong, in some way, to a particular deity. Eating almost anything meant eating food offered to gods—or, from a Christian perspective, to the idols. What then were Christians to do? The Corinthian query is this: We now realize that there is only one God; can we therefore eat anything and

The Origin of 1 Corinthians (Macon, GA: Mercer University Press, 2nd edn, 1983 [1965]).

not fear that we are being polluted by idols? Here is Paul's response: In theory, you are quite right: 'we know that "no idol in the world really exists", and that "there is no God but one"' (8.4). In practice, however, not all Christians have rid themselves fully of their beliefs in other gods. Rather than insist on your right to eat anything you want and force others to adhere to that principle, it is best to be sensitive to other Christians' insecurities (8.7-12). So, I recommend that you restrict your freedom, even to the point of abstaining from certain foods, so as not to disturb the consciences of the 'weaker' Christians (8.13; also 10.23-30).

This Pauline perspective is consistent with his advice on sex in ch. 7: in both cases he shows respect for the views of others and does not insist that they adhere to his principles. He restates his position on dietary practices in Rom. 14.17: 'For the kingdom of God is not food and drink but righteousness and peace and joy in the Holy Spirit'.

Paul's stance continues in 1 Corinthians 12–14, where he addresses the issue of spiritual gifts. The question here concerns how the Corinthians are to determine whether one of their members has a 'spiritual gift' (charisma) and whether 'speaking in tongues' is the most valuable of these gifts. Paul argues as follows. In theory, speaking in tongues is a wonderful gift, one that I possess myself, as you well know (14.18). But in practice we should recognize and appreciate the diversity of spiritual gifts (listed in 12.8-10, 28-30) and strive to support those gifts that bring the community together rather than those that separate it—by either being incomprehensible or claiming special status. Appreciating the value of each other's gifts— 'loving' one another (ch. 13)—is worth more than anything. Hence, Paul's perspective on this issue, as with the others, underlines his belief that unity in his communities is paramount and must be based on an appreciation of each person's contribution to the whole. Christians, in Paul's mind, are all worthy members of the 'body of Christ' (1 Cor. 12.14-27):

> Indeed, the body does not consist of one member but of many. If the foot would say, 'Because I am not a hand, I do not belong to the body,' that would not make it any less a part of the body. And if the ear would say, 'Because I am not an eye, I do not belong to the body,' that would not make it any less a part of the body. If the whole body were an eye, where would the hearing be? If the whole body were hearing, where would the sense of smell be? But as it is, God arranged the members in the body, each one of them, as he chose. If all were a single member, where would

the body be? As it is, there are many members, yet one body. The eye cannot say to the hand, 'I have no need of you,' nor again the head to the feet, 'I have no need of you.' On the contrary, the members of the body that seem to be weaker are indispensable, and those members of the body that we think less honorable we clothe with greater honor, and our less respectable members are treated with greater respect; whereas our more respectable members do not need this. But God has so arranged the body, giving the greater honor to the inferior member, that there may be no dissension within the body, but the members may have the same care for one another. If one member suffers, all suffer together with it; if one member is honored, all rejoice together with it. Now you are the body of Christ and individually members of it.

This text brings us back full circle to Paul's ideal of equality. His spirit of compromise is based on the belief that baptism has a trans-formative power, which turns everyone into a part of the 'body of Christ', making each person an equal child of God. In the Pastorals especially (e.g., 1 Tim. 3.15) 'the household of God' to which all Christians belong becomes the operative metaphor. This perception lies at the heart of Paul's willingness to compromise and his insistence on equality. Paul expresses it forcefully in his letters, and this view is essentially peace-promoting. How can one inflict violence on another part of one's own body?

7. Summary

The New Testament advocates peace. The one hundred direct refer-ences to the term itself suggest an importance which is borne out on several levels. What must first be noted is the explicit anti-violence message. Christians in the New Testament are never called upon to make war on other human beings. There is no call to arms. Instead, they are required to make peace and are called blessed if they do. According to Luke, Jesus considers a disciple to be a 'child of peace' (10.6). God, as Paul repeatedly says, is the 'God of peace', and Jesus is called 'our peace' because he reconciled people to God through his death, not through the killing of others.

The message of peace is distributed widely. Some of the sayings attributed to Jesus transmit that message directly (e.g., 'all who take the sword will perish by the sword'—Mt. 26.52), as do some of Paul's directives to his companion Timothy ('a bishop must be…not violent but gentle'—1 Tim. 3.3) and to the Roman Christians ('let every person be subject to the governing authorities'—Rom. 13.1). What reinforces this New Testament teaching most effectively, though, is the way it is lived out by the first generation of Christians as they appear in the pages of the New Testament. The book of Acts presents peaceful individuals as models to emulate—especially in its leading characters Simon Peter and Paul. The Acts viewpoint in turn coheres with the impression of Jesus created in the Gospels.

Coupled with this clear prohibition against violence is a willingness to accept it from others, even to the point of death. This acceptance of other people's violence is in fact the dominant message, and it is expressed in a variety of ways. Mark, for instance, in his Gospel creatively organizes the treatment of Jesus and his disciples to reinforce the impression that Jesus' messiahship can only be defined in terms of suffering and death, and that those closest to him failed to understand this while he was alive. The book of Revelation makes martyrdom all that more attractive by projecting a special thousand-year transitory age available only for martyrs, to be spent with Jesus (20.4-6). A double-edged exhortation emerges, then, from the New Testament: do not be violent toward others and do be willing to suffer the violence of others, following Jesus' example and that set by his earliest followers.

The violence that is to be embraced and withheld is not only physical in nature. The New Testament constantly encourages its readers and listeners to open themselves to a new appreciation of their own needs and the needs of others. The Sermon on the Mount seeks this end plainly, whereas the parables perhaps achieve it best. 'Be little ones' is the New Testament refrain: be forgiving and humble, open to treating every Christian as an equal. Give people the freedom to make up their own minds (as the parable genre reinforces and as Paul often does in his own communities). And do not forget the basic human needs of your Christian brothers and sisters (e.g., in James). These are all peace-promoting exhortations.

The New Testament insists that this radical perspective was instilled during baptism, reinforced by the teachings of the early churches, and kept vividly alive by the expectation of an imminent end to this world, to be followed by divine judgment for all. These signs indicate that the peace message was taken quite seriously by the earliest Christians. We know that the message has continued to resonate with varying degrees of intensity throughout the centuries.

Chapter 3

VIOLENCE IN THE NEW TESTAMENT

The strong New Testament message of peace should not blind us to the fact that these books are also suffused with violence. To a certain extent, this violence mirrors the human condition that naturally exists in every century. It also includes the sufferings inflicted on Jesus and his followers. The issue goes much further than this, however, for the New Testament also promotes violence. Given this situation, it is legitimate to ask whether we are not faced with a *trompe l'oeil*, an optical illusion where the same picture can, for example, look like a vase one moment and two opposite silhouettes of faces the next. The collection of New Testament texts remains the same, but the expectations or the points of focus allow images of peace and violence to appear and disappear in turn.

The violent dimension sometimes takes time to see. My intent in this chapter is to present the textual evidence which supports the existence of the New Testament's violent side. I begin, as in Chapter 2, by describing the vocabulary associated with this issue, providing an overview of some of the features which contribute a violent flavour to the New Testament. Then I turn to four aspects that reinforce this violent perspective. The first is the New Testament's unquestioning acceptance of soldiers and war. The second concerns the authors' fascination with the extreme violence that is expected to occur at the very end of this age, including the wrath of God inflicted on humanity. The male domination of these texts provides the third type of violent perspective. The fourth is the tendency to group humanity into camps of 'insiders' and 'outsiders'. In this examination of the many forms in which violence manifests itself in the New Testament, non-physical violence predominates.

1. *The Vocabulary*

The strategy of isolating and defining the explicit uses of 'peace' in the previous chapter had its advantages and disadvantages. The common occurrence of such language suggested an importance that was borne out in a more wide-ranging study, but not all references to peace were relevant to our subject matter; additionally, some important peace-promoting sections of the New Testament (e.g., the Sermon on the Mount) contain virtually no specific references to the word 'peace'. The same can be said for the words relating to violence, with the added problem in this case that it is not as obvious which words to include. Acts, for instance, presents what is essentially a peaceful development of early Christianity, yet its stories refer frequently to violence, arrests, and the like. On the other hand, letters such as Galatians and 2 Peter, which evince considerable anger against dissident Christians, lack words such as 'violence', 'war' or 'sword'. One cannot assume that references to 'peace' necessarily result in a peaceful book, and vice versa. It still helps, however, to get an overview of the relevant vocabulary. Words do matter.

Many terms in the New Testament raise the spectre of violence.[1]

1.   The key terms and locations are as follows:

bia (force, violence): Acts 5.26; 21.35; 27.41 [3X];
biazesthai (to apply force): Mt. 11.12; 16.16 [2X];
biaios (violent, forcible): Acts 2.22 [1X];
biastes (a violent person): Mt. 11.12 [1X];
hormema (a violent rush, an onset): Rev. 18.21 [1X];
diasein (to extort money by violence): Lk. 3.14 [1X];
polemein (to wage war, fight): Jas 4.7; Rev. 2.16; 12.7, 7; 13.4; 17.14; 19.11 [7X];
polemos (a war, a fight): Mt. 24.6, 6; Mk 13.7; Lk. 14.31; 21.9; 1 Cor. 14.8; Heb.
    11.34; Jas 4.1; Rev. 9.7, 9; 11.7; 12.7, 17; 13.7; 16.14; 19.19; 20.8 [17X];
mache (a battle, a quarrel): 2 Cor. 7.5; 2 Tim. 2.23; Tit. 3.9; Jas 4.1 [4X];
machomai (to fight, to quarrel): Jn 6.52; Acts 7.26; 2 Tim. 2.24; Jas 4.2 [4X];
strateuesthai (to do military service): Lk. 3.14; 1 Cor. 9.7; 2 Cor. 10.3; 1 Tim. 1.18,
    18; 2 Tim. 2.4; Jas 4.1; 1 Pet. 2.11 [8X];
stratia (an army): Lk. 2.13; Acts 7.42 [2X];
stratiotes (a soldier): Mt. 8.9; 27.27; 28.12; Mk 15.16; Lk. 7.8; 23.36; Jn 19.2, 23, 23,
    25, 32, 34; Acts 10.7; 12.4, 6, 18; 21.32, 32, 35; 23.23, 31; 27.31, 32, 42; 28.16; 2
    Tim. 2.3 [26X];
sustratiotes (a fellow soldier): Phlm. 2; Phil. 2.25 [2X];
stratopedon (a body of troops): Lk. 21.20 [1X];
strateuma (an army): Mt. 22.7; Lk. 23.11; Acts 23.10, 27; Rev. 9.16; 19.14, 19, 19 [8X];
strateia (a military campaign): 2 Cor. 10.4; 1 Tim. 1.18 [2X];
stratologein (to gather an army, enlist): 2 Tim. 2.4 [1X];

Words connected in a general way with violence are not common—
for instance, *bia* (force, violence), *biazesthai* (to apply force), *biaios*
(violent, forcible), *biastes* (a violent person), *hormema* (a violent
rush) and *diasein* (to extort money by violence, or 'shake down') occur
only nine times in all. General words for quarrelling and fighting are
somewhat more frequent: *polemein* and *machomesthai* (both mean 'to
fight') and their noun forms *polemos* and *mache* occur collectively 32
times. Military vocabulary is what dominates. Throughout the New
Testament one frequently encounters (97 times) armies (*stratia*,
strateuma), military campaigns (*strateia*) and the gathering of armies
(*stratologein*); people serving in the army (*strateuesthai*) and battling
with other armies (*antistrateuesthai*); and troops (*stratopedon*), weapons
and armour (*thorax*, *perikephala*, *panoplia*, *thureos*, *machaira*,
romphaia), soldiers (*stratiotes*) and fellow soldiers (*sustratiotes*). The
presence of these terms, to a large extent, is a reflection of the
military environment in which first-century Christians lived. They do
not exhaust the vocabulary that could be included in a discussion about
violence, but they do give a sense of the range of possibilities.

The terms are widely-dispersed. Three quarters are found in the
Gospels (46), Acts (23) and Revelation (33) combined, the books which
most directly explore the Christian involvement with the political
and religious authorities. Only one fifth (27) are found in the Pauline
corpus.[2] They are entirely absent from eight letters (Galatians,
Colossians, 2 Thessalonians, 2 Peter, 1–3 John, Jude). Overall, terms
for violence, while not having as wide a distribution as 'peace', occur
frequently throughout most of the New Testament.

The terms tend to be used in three ways. The first refers to physical
human violence, usually inflicted on Christians but sometimes by
Christians themselves on others. In Rom. 3.35, for example, Paul

---

antistrateuesthai (to war against): Rom. 7.23 [1×];
thorax (a breastplate): Eph. 6.14;1 Thess. 5.8; Rev. 9.9, 9, 17 [5×];
perikephalaia (a helmet): Eph. 6.17; 1 Thess. 5.8 [2×];
panoplia (full armour): Lk. 11.22; Eph. 6.11, 13 [3×];
thureos (a long oblong shield): Eph. 6.16 [1×];
machaira (a sword): Mt. 10.34; 26.47, 51, 52, 52, 55; Mk 14.43, 47, 48; Lk. 21.24;
    22.36, 38, 49, 52; Jn 18.10, 11; Acts 12.2, 16.27; Rom. 8.35; 13.4; Eph. 6.17;
    Heb. 4.12; 11.34, 37; Rev. 6.4; 13.10, 10, 14 [28×];
romphaia (a sword, a sabre): Lk. 2.35; Rev. 1.16; 2.12, 16; 6.8; 19.15, 21 [7×].

---

2.   These terms are distributed fairly evenly throughout the Pauline corpus
between the undisputed letters (twelve times) and the disputed ones (fifteen times).

states that even 'the sword' (i.e., violent arrest) should not interfere with one's life as a Christian, while later in the same letter he encourages his community to be law-abiding lest they be punished 'by the sword' (Rom. 13.4). In Jn 18.10 Simon Peter cuts off the ear of the high priest's slave with his sword. Several passages (e.g., Mk 13.7; Mt. 24.6) anticipate pitched battles in the end times. This context provides a second kind of use for these terms, for what is expected then is violent encounters between the forces of good and the forces of evil. 'The Beast', we are told, will wage war against God (e.g., Rev. 11.7; 13.7; 16.14) and God and his heavenly agents will reciprocate (Rev. 2.16; 19.11). These battles are thought to be quite real, but the weapons used are not physical in nature. Hence, God will come to make war 'with the sword of his mouth' (Rev. 2.16), and Paul informs us that Jesus will slay 'the lawless one…with the breath of his mouth' (2 Thess. 2.8).

The third way the terms are used is metaphorical. This usage is the most common. Military strength and activity become metaphors for a Christian's readiness to withstand anything for God. Paul in particular enjoys using these military metaphors. 'Let us be sober, and put on the breastplate of faith and love, and for a helmet the hope of salvation', he exhorts the Thessalonians (1 Thess. 5.8; expanded in Eph. 6.10-18). 'If a bugle gives an indistinct sound, who will get ready for battle', he says to the Corinthians (1 Cor. 14.8), encouraging them to prepare for their spiritual battles by speaking words intelligible by all. Moreover, his co-workers are called 'fellow soldiers' (Archippus in Phlm. 2; Epaphroditus in Phil. 2.25), and in 2 Tim. 2.3-6 all Christians are compared to 'good soldiers of Jesus Christ'. Indeed, the title of the well-known hymn, 'Onward Christian Soldiers', while not taken literally from the New Testament, certainly has a New Testament ring to it.

The New Testament terms for violence, therefore, express different levels of reality. A sword is not always a sword, and all battles are not alike. To simplify: the sword that cuts off the ear of the high priest's slave is a real sword in a real skirmish; the one that is expected to slay 'the lawless one' and the one which the author of Ephesians includes as part of a Christian's armour (6.10-17) are symbolic swords in struggles against evil. This range of usage suggests already some of the complexities inherent in understanding the New Testament perspective on violence.

2. *An Overview of the Violent Exhortations and Actions*

Throughout the New Testament Jesus and his followers can be found accepting, condoning, and even inciting violence. This section highlights two features which reinforce that perspective. The first is the angry, self-righteous tone that can be heard throughout the New Testament; the second is the assumption that violence is sometimes necessary to effect positive changes. Together, these features begin to suggest how this overtly peace-promoting collection of documents has so often been used to support violence against others.

a. *The Tone*

The angry tone found in much of the New Testament can best be appreciated by first putting it in context. Two historical factors in particular help to account for this tone: the Jewish roots of early Christianity and the Christians' lack of success in convincing most others of the truth of their claims. The Jewish matrix is important. Christianity emerged directly out of Judaism. Jesus, his twelve disciples and Paul were all Jews who considered their faith to be consistent with Judaism. Almost all the books which later became part of the New Testament were composed by Jews who had come to believe that Jesus was their long-awaited Messiah, that his death ushered in the beginning of the end, and that humanity's only hope for avoiding eternal damnation was to accept Jesus as son of God before the end overtook them. Christians applied the Jewish claim of chosen status to themselves, and to some extent democratized it: 'chosenness' now applied not only to one race, but was open to all. Moreover, 'getting into' the religion and 'staying in' were simplified (e.g., male converts did not have to undergo circumcision). Yet a fundamental assumption remained the same: outsiders faced misfortune and, likely, eternal damnation. The Christian motto might have been: 'there is salvation in no one else' but Jesus (Acts 4.12).

The second contributing factor was the increasing failure of Christian missionary activities. After the initial wave of excitement preceding and following Jesus' death, the Jesus movement did not make large inroads into either Judaism or the rest of the Greco-Roman world. It did not die, which itself is remarkable, but it certainly grew more slowly than Christians hoped—and expected in light of what they perceived to be the imminent end. A reading of Acts might suggest otherwise, for that book emphasizes the numerical growth of Christianity during the three decades following Jesus' death: 'about three thousand persons were added' (2.41) after the Pentecost, 'five thousand' more a short time later (4.4), and so forth. Advertising the growth of the Christian movement is precisely what Acts sets out to do, but even this book admits in its closing verses that very early on the Jews for the most part rejected that message. Romans 9–11 restates that very point and agonizes over what could have led to such a situation. As well, the success among non-Jews not only remained unspectacular during the span of time depicted in Acts, but even declined afterwards. Telling proof comes from the correspondence of Pliny the Younger, who was sent from Rome to govern the Asian province of Bithynia in 111 CE. Pliny was a well-educated Roman citizen with a particular interest in philosophical and religious matters. When he encountered a group of Christians in his new province he asked the emperor Trajan for guidance because he had no idea who Christians were or what he should do with them. This anecdote helps to show that the vision held by Peter and Paul of Christians converting the world was certainly not realized during the time in which the books of the New Testament were written.[3]

The early Christians believed that they had access to the truth—God's truth—in spite of many factors which might have suggested otherwise: their leader Jesus had been put to death, branded as a failed revolutionary; their missionary activities met with less and less favour; Jesus' return kept being delayed; and both Jews and Romans remained powerful. Indeed, from a first-century non-Christian perspective, Christians appeared as losers who thought of themselves as winners. Christian missionaries at the end of the first century likely

---

3.   Christians, however, were far from invisible throughout the first century. Two incidents noted by Roman historians suggest that Christians in the middle of the century attracted attention in the capital city. Under Nero (*ca.* 64 CE) Christians in Rome were blamed for setting a major fire in the city, and many were put to death. The historians who recount the incident (Tacitus, *Annals*, 15.44; Suetonius, *Nero*, 16) are not fond of Nero; they claim that the charges were fabricated. Also, about 50 CE the Jewish Christians (or some of them) seem to have been expelled by the emperor Claudius. Suetonius (*Claudius*, 25) recounts that incident, but his ambiguous phrasing makes it impossible to reconstruct what actually took place. Acts 18.1-2 merely states it as a fact: 'After this Paul left Athens and went to Corinth. There he found a Jew named Aquila, a native of Pontus, who had recently come from Italy with his wife Priscilla, because Claudius had ordered all Jews to leave Rome.'

received as much respect from outsiders as the Jehovah's Witnesses do today when they knock on doors. Given this situation, it is not surprising to find a certain seriousness and desperation to the Christian preaching. There is virtually no humour or joking in the New Testament. Nor is it surprising to witness the occasional outbursts of resentment and self-righteous indignation.

Paul is one Christian who occasionally felt free to express his anger and frustration openly. His letters address issues and problems dear to him and to his communities. In several of them Paul reveals a recurring problem: other Christians have visited his churches and preached a slightly different version of the Christian message. They argued—with some success, it would appear, and apparently with the support of some of the Christian leaders in Jerusalem—that Christianity is a form of Judaism requiring its members to adhere to some of the Jewish legal requirements (e.g., circumcision for males; and, according to Acts 15.19-21, some dietary restrictions).[4] Paul not only disagrees with this preaching (e.g., 1 Cor. 7.17-20), but lashes out angrily at those preachers whom he labels 'false Christians'. In Gal. 1.9 he curses his doctrinal enemies: 'If anyone proclaims to you a gospel contrary to what you received, let that one be accursed!' In that same letter he also compares himself positively to Peter, upon whom his opponents probably based some of their claims (2.11-16), and wishes that the person who circumcised them when they became Christians (or Jews) would have castrated himself instead (5.12). There is more. In 2 Cor. 11.5 Paul sarcastically refers to these Christian missionaries as 'superapostles', and in Philippians (3.2) he warns the community to 'beware of the dogs, beware of the evil workers, beware of those who mutilate the flesh'. This is harsh language, especially when one considers that Paul is addressing his fellow Christians. This model of human interaction that Paul presents is not particularly peace-promoting: on certain issues compromise is possible and even encouraged, but on other issues there can be no compromise. Simply put, Paul believes that he has 'the mind of Christ' (1 Cor. 2.16) and that those who disagree with him over this, and

4.   The beginning of Galatians clearly suggests that Paul wants uppermost to ground his teachings and authority directly in a revelation from Jesus. When that is fixed in his readers' minds, he goes on to say that he received the stamp of approval from Peter and James, one of Jesus' brothers (1.18-24). This apparently furthers his case against his opponents who seem to claim the same human support.

over other fundamental tenets, are wrong and accursed. He vents his anger upon them with impunity. This model of dealing with dissident Christians continues in other New Testament letters, most notably 2 Peter, Jude and 1 John.

This Pauline model has its precedent in the Gospels' presentations of Jesus. Paul might believe that he has 'the mind of Christ', but the evangelists, of course, believe that Jesus is the Christ. They write their Gospels in order to convince others of this belief. In their eyes, Jesus cannot be wrong and he can do no wrong…and, especially according to Matthew and John, woe to those who suggest otherwise! In John, those who doubt Jesus' authority are 'the Jews', and they become the human foils for Jesus' divinity. Jesus toys with them throughout the narrative and condemns them unequivocally: 'You are from your father the devil' (8.44). Not only are they cast relentlessly as Jesus' opponents in John's Gospel, 'the Jews' are considered by nature evil and unredeemable. In Matthew, 'the Pharisees' are the doubting group. Jesus also taunts them throughout this Gospel. No Pharisee can be a good Pharisee. This depiction climaxes in Jesus' vituperative out-burst in ch. 23. 'Woe to you, scribes and Pharisees, hypocrites!' he declares six times (23.13, 16—with variation: 23.23, 25, 27, 29) and ends with: 'You snakes, you brood of vipers! How can you escape being sentenced to hell?' (23.33). In 27.24-25 hatred directed against this particular group even spreads to the entire nation when the evangelist insists that all the Jewish people condemned Jesus to death. They and their descendants from that time on deserve whatever they get in return for this:

> So when Pilate saw that he could do nothing, but rather that a riot was beginning, he took some water and washed his hands before the crowd, saying, 'I am innocent of this man's blood; see to it yourselves.' Then the people as a whole answered, 'His blood be on us and on our children!'

The only redeeming factor to these verses is that the author himself was Jewish.[5]

The anger and resentment voiced by all the New Testament writers is often directed either at Jews, since they made Jesus' life difficult and continued to be a major source of aggravation for Christians after his death, or at 'Judaizers', that is, Christians who insisted on closer links

---

5. Christian anti-Semitism over the centuries finds much of its biblical support in these verses.

with Judaism than Paul (especially) thought necessary. The Christians' lack of success in the mission fields may have contributed to the frustration, as would the mere proximity of the early Christian communities to their Jewish brethren. The tone, then, is understandable, given the historical context, but the violence remains.

b. *The Occasional Acceptance of Violence*
The New Testament view is that violence is sometimes required to effect positive changes. The agent is usually God, but it can be Jesus acting as God's representative. Occasionally it is a Christian. This position helps to reinforce a structure of conflict resolution which depends on force as a primary principle, regardless of who inflicts the violence (Christians rarely do).

A great deal of violence is attributed to God throughout the New Testament. Occasionally he inflicts suffering on humans in order to toughen them: 'I reprove and discipline those whom I love', is his claim in Rev. 3.19. The author of Hebrews exhorts his group not to despair over these kinds of 'fatherly' actions (12.7-11):

> Endure trials for the sake of discipline. God is treating you as children; for what child is there whom a parent does not discipline? If you do not have that discipline in which all children share, then you are illegitimate and not his children. Moreover, we had human parents to discipline us, and we respected them. Should we not be even more willing to be subject to the Father of spirits and live? For they disciplined us for a short time as seemed best to them, but he disciplines us for our good, in order that we may share his holiness. Now, discipline always seems painful rather than pleasant at the time, but later it yields the peaceful fruit of righteousness to those who have been trained in it.

Human sickness must be considered part of this suffering, for sickness was thought to be caused primarily by sin. In other words, God was responsible for afflicting people who did not meet with his approval, and only harmony (at-one-ment) with him could treat the real causes of any sickness. Treating the symptoms was futile. Jn 5.14 exhibits this common first-century Jewish perspective, and Jn 9.1-3 presents a fascinating twist to it. In chapter nine Jesus and his disciples encounter a man who has been born blind. This leads the disciples to ask a logical question, given the presupposition that sin leads to illness: 'Rabbi, who sinned, this man or his parents, that he was born blind?' Jesus, as he does throughout this Gospel, gives an unexpected answer: 'Neither this man nor his parents sinned; he was born blind so that

God's works might be revealed in him.' In other words, the man was born blind in anticipation of Jesus' miracle. This story plainly reveals the point of view that human misfortune is at least partly in God's hands.

Occasionally God kills those who act against his wishes. The most explicit example occurs in Acts 5.1-11, a passage in which a husband and then his wife are killed outright, apparently by God acting through Peter, for not giving up all their property to the Christian community as they had declared:

> But a man Ananias, with the consent of his wife Sapphira, sold a piece of property; with his wife's knowledge, he kept back some of the proceeds, and brought only a part and laid it at the apostles' feet. 'Ananias,' Peter asked, 'why has Satan filled your heart to lie to the Holy Spirit and to keep back part of the proceeds of the land? While it remained unsold, did it not remain your own? And after it was sold, were not the proceeds at your disposal? How is it that you have contrived this deed in your heart? You did not lie to us but to God!' Now when Ananias heard these words, he fell down and died. And great fear seized all who heard of it. The young men came and wrapped up his body, then carried him out and buried him. After an interval of about three hours his wife came in, not knowing what had happened. Peter said to her, 'Tell me whether you and your husband sold the land for such and such a price.' And she said, 'Yes, that was the price.' Then Peter said to her, 'How is it that you have agreed together to put the Spirit of the Lord to the test? Look, the feet of those who have buried your husband are at the door, and they will carry you out.' Immediately she fell down at his feet and died. When the young men came in they found her dead, so they carried her out and buried her beside her husband. And great fear seized the whole church and all who heard of these things.

Nor do the punishments end when a person dies, for on Judgment day God is expected to reward some and punish others. The punishments are feared. Several parables allude to these coming horrors. One is the Wedding Banquet in Mt. 22.1-14, which ends with an image of the punishments awaiting a Christian who has not remained faithful: '"Bind him hand and foot, and throw him into the outer darkness, where there will be weeping and gnashing of teeth." For many are called but few are chosen.' Luke 12.41-48 also presents a model for how God treats wayward Christians (especially Christian leaders) after their death. This parable states that a 'slave' who is not ready for the 'master's' arrival will be beaten, but a 'slave who knew what his master wanted' but did not respond (i.e., a Christian who knows God's wishes) will receive a more severe beating. It concludes: 'From every one to whom much has been given, much will be required; and from the one to whom much has been entrusted, even more will be demanded' (12.48). The author of Hebrews starkly expresses this common New Testament belief (10.26-31): 'For if we willfully persist in sin after having received the knowledge of the truth, there no longer remains a sacrifice for sins, but a fearful prospect of judgment, and a fury of fire that will consume the adversaries.' The threat of punishment hangs over the Christian's head. Moreover, the violence that is expressly forbidden of humans is placed in God's lap. Put simply, people are not to inflict violence on others because that is God's domain: 'vengeance is mine, I will repay' (Rom. 12.19). What is more, God is expected to react to the evil forces with extreme violence. Early Christians believed: 'the God of peace will soon crush Satan under your feet' (Rom. 16.20). Several passages (e.g., 2 Thess. 2; Mk 13; Mt. 24; Lk. 21) and an entire book (Revelation) describe the carnage that will ensue. The world is not expected to 'go gently into that dark night', for the end will be frightfully violent. God imposes suffering and death on Jesus as well. The 'peace' that is offered to humans is effected through the violence which God allows to come upon Jesus. Throughout the New Testament, God's violence is considered necessary to make people better, to give them more direct access to the divine, to reward them fairly after they die, and to rid the world of evil. It is not considered evil.

Viewed as God's agent on earth (or his ambassador to humanity), Jesus himself occasionally accepts, condones, or incites violence. Partly, this is because he is depicted as choosing to involve himself in social, political and religious issues rather than, for instance, escaping to the shores of the Dead Sea to live a monastic existence with the Essenes.[6] Yet the way he involves himself inevitably leads to trouble,

---

6. The Essenes were Jews who, in protest against what they perceived as religious laxity and corruption in their day, chose to separate themselves from the rest of their people and live a monastic existence on the shores of the Dead Sea. Little is known about their origins. They may have emerged shortly after the Maccabean revolt (167–164 BCE), when the new Jewish state failed to live up to the conservative religious ideals of some of the rebels. The last of their members appear to have been killed at Masada during the Jewish war against Rome in 66–73 CE. Some of the 'Dead Sea Scrolls', discovered in 1947, testify to this form of Jewish religiosity. The Essenes were well-known in the first century. They exhibit many similarities with the early Christian communities (e.g., they had their own 'Teacher of Righteousness'

and eventually to his arrest and execution. The New Testament Jesus would have had to have been a fool not to foresee the violent consequences of some of his actions, at least as they are described in the Gospels. In the much-debated question of who or what was responsible for Jesus' death, Jesus himself must surely bear at least some of the blame.

Several sayings present Jesus as intent on disrupting people's lives. According to Matthew 10.34-36, he states:

> Do not think that I have come to bring peace to the earth; I have not come to bring peace but a sword. For I have come to set a man against his father, and a daughter against her mother, and a daughter-in-law against her mother-in-law; and one's foes will be members of one's own household.[7]

The commitment expected of his followers entails not only pitting family members against one another, but abandoning the family model altogether. Disciples are not encouraged to be faithful to their families (Mk 3.31-35; Lk. 8.19-21; Mt. 12.46-50). Loyalty to the religious group takes precedence even over the custom to show respect for dead family members by burying them (Mt. 8.19-22; Lk. 9.57-67). One cannot expect to preach this sort of message with impunity. The Christian apocryphal Acts, written during the second and third centuries, describe the journeys of various apostles, and deal precisely with the large number of violent incidents that arose when Christians attempted to live strictly by this model. They describe groups of itinerant Christians who renounced worldly possessions, as well as sexual activity of any kind, and encouraged others to do likewise. Non-Christians understandably were angered by the loss of their children or their spouses to what they saw as a strange cult, and violence ensued.

Jesus' teaching on whether his followers had to pay taxes would have also caused him trouble—more than modern readers of the New Testament often realize. The Markan version is as follows (for the parallel versions see Mt. 22.15-22; Lk. 20.20-26):

and expected the end time to come soon).

7.   The parallel text in Luke 12.51-53 substitutes 'division' for 'sword', but the meaning is not altered. This saying has nothing to do with Jesus encouraging physical violence (with a sword!). It still has to be asked, though, to what extent Jesus' attitude would have contributed to the violence of others.

> Then they sent to him some Pharisees and some Herodians to trap him in what he said. And they came and said to him, 'Teacher, we know that you are sincere, and show deference to no one; for you do not regard people with partiality, but teach the way of God in accordance with truth. Is it lawful to pay taxes to the emperor, or not? Should we pay them, or should we not?' But knowing their hypocrisy, he said to them, 'Why are you putting me to the test? Bring me a denarius and let me see it.' And they brought one. Then he said to them, 'Whose head is this, and whose title?' They answered, 'The emperor's.' Jesus said to them, 'Give to the emperor the things that are the emperor's, and to God the things that are God's.' And they were utterly amazed at him.

For many churchgoers today this story has come to symbolize the compatibility of Christianity to the world: pay your taxes and perform your other civic duties, but devote the rest of your time to God. New Testament interpreters, however, have long recognized that the trap set for Jesus in this story is effective only if it provides him with a dilemma. Otherwise there is little at which to be 'utterly amazed'. Many 'Third World' readers and hearers of this story now also recognize the tension and see Jesus' response as revolutionary. What is at issue? If Jesus answers, 'No, don't pay your taxes', he will be arrested. That is obvious. What is not as obvious is that if he answers, 'Yes, pay your taxes', he is also in trouble—probably because he stands to lose face with at least a sizeable number of his followers.

This dilemma is all the more likely if those followers, perhaps including Jesus himself, were part of the underground Jewish resistance movement so prevalent during the first century. The resistance fighters about which we have some information certainly did not shirk from using violence to rid the nation of the dreaded occupation troops and the Roman demand for taxes on what was seen as God's land. Hence, for the early audiences of the Gospels, this story would have carried with it undertones of violence and physical resistance. Those audiences would have smiled at Jesus' response ('Give to the emperor the things that are the emperor's, and to God the things that are God's'), for many believed that everything belonged to God and nothing to the emperor. Jesus' answer, therefore, is quite fitting because it means different things to different audiences, pleasing all (except those who wished to entrap Jesus). It is not surprising to read, in the Lukan charges brought against Jesus before Pilate (Lk. 23.1-2), that one of these three includes the accusation of forbidding Jews from paying taxes to the emperor. When read through first-century (or twentieth-century 'Third World') eyes, this New Testament story points in the direction of an openness on Jesus' part to condoning violence.

Two of Jesus' actions are even more charged with violence. The first is what the Gospels present as a grand entrance into Jerusalem during the Festival of Passover (Mk 11.1-10; Mt. 21.1-9; Lk. 19.28-30). To be sure, the entry is said to be non-violent, but its historical context has to be kept in mind in order to appreciate the full force of such an action. Passover, for Jews, symbolized freedom—the escape of the Israelites from Egypt centuries before, and since that time, freedom from all foreign oppression. Emotions ran high during this festival, a time when all Jews tried to visit Jerusalem. Indeed, emotions ran so high that the Romans would keep the high priest's sacred vestments locked up then, lest the people rise up and declare him their political leader. The Gospels themselves show awareness of the charged nature of this festival. We read in Mk 14.1-2 (see also Mt. 26.1-5):

> It was two days before the Passover and the festival of Unleavened Bread. The chief priests and the scribes were looking for a way to arrest Jesus by stealth and kill him; for they said, 'Not during the festival, or there may be a riot among the people.'

Jesus' entry into Jerusalem during Passover, preceded as it was by his reputation as a teacher and miracle worker, needed little more to ensure a violent outcome.

If his entry did not cause one, the temple incident of the following day certainly would have (Mk 11.15-19; Mt. 21.12-13; Lk. 19.45-48; Jn 2.13-17).[8] In Luke's account Jesus is said to enter the temple, where he 'began to drive out those who were selling things there'. According to Matthew and Mark his entry is accompanied by the overturning of the tables and seats of the vendors and money changers.[9] John even more pointedly says that Jesus made a whip of

8.   The chronology of this incident comes from the Synoptic accounts. John places the incident early in Jesus' career, apparently to typify Jesus' mission as a symbol for the thorough 'cleansing' of Judaism.

9.   Money changers provided a valuable service by allowing visitors to exchange their native coins for those required by the temple (to pay the priests, buy food and sacrificial animals, etc.). Those people selling animals also played an important role. Temple service revolved around offering animals to God (for thanks, redemption, etc.), and these offerings had to be 'without blemish' according to biblical law (Lev. 1.3). So it made sense to buy the animals from recognized authorities. The buying and selling of animals went on in the outer courtyard of the temple, which was open

cords and drove out the animals and some of the people.

The scholarly debate over whether this particular incident actually occurred, especially in the manner recounted by (one of) the evangelists, or whether it is best understood as a theological statement dressed in historical garb, influences the amount of violence that one attributes to the historical Jesus.[10] My concern in this study, however, lies not in unearthing the historical Jesus (an irresolvable issue, in any case), but in appreciating the New Testament presentation of him.

The evangelists all include this incident. They do so primarily to state their perception of the degeneration of Jewish religious practices, and perhaps also to prefigure the coming destruction of the temple. Not to be forgotten in each of these accounts is Jesus' apparent willingness to use violence (albeit minimally) in order to make his point.[11] More important, the way the story is presented makes it difficult to imagine Jesus not expecting a violent reaction to his attack on the holy precinct. In fact, according to the Synoptic narratives, his arrest is said to follow shortly after this incident. Only modern audiences unaware of the real-life situation of first-century Palestine and nurtured on the image of a peaceful Jesus can read this story and not see violence occurring and about to occur. To be fair, not many of Jesus' actions fall under this category.

The same can be said about his followers. One surprising feature, for instance, is that occasionally Jesus' followers carried weapons while they travelled. This point is not emphasized by the evangelists, but two stories bring it to light. The first is Jesus' arrest. All four Gospels state that at Jesus' arrest one of his companions drew his sword,

---

to all. The temple became increasingly restrictive as one moved inwards, excluding in turn non-Jews, women, non-priests; finally only the high priest was allowed to enter the 'holy of holies' once a year.

10. Some scholars, for instance, have seen the narration of the story as the tip of an iceberg of violent activity, suggesting that Jesus and his followers were political revolutionaries whose violent proclivities were downplayed by the evangelists. Many have expressed serious reservations about an incident occurring in this manner, since the temple precincts were heavily guarded: it would have taken far more than a single individual, armed with a whip or not, to create a large disturbance and then walk away from it. For a recent survey of opinions and a new perspective, see Sanders, *Jesus and Judaism*, pp. 61-76.

11. The Essene Teacher of Righteousness made essentially the same point peacefully by removing himself and his followers from Jerusalem and the temple as a form of protest. Jesus, the Gospels tell us, did not hesitate to confront the authorities violently.

struck the slave of the High Priest and cut off his ear (Mk 14.43-52; Mt. 26.47-56; Lk. 22.47-53; Jn 18.2-11). John identifies this figure as Simon Peter. In all four cases the context suggests nothing unusual about one of Jesus' companions having a sword. In fact, the accounts suggest that most, if not all of them, were armed. They do not say, 'one of his companions had a sword', but 'one of those who stood near drew his sword' (Mk 14.47). How is Jesus said to react? Mark does not record any reaction at all to this violent act—Jesus is neither offended nor pleased. The other three evangelists express Jesus' disapproval in different ways and include a scenario to explain the swords. Scholars debate which version of this story is the earliest, and what part of it, if any, goes back to the historical Jesus. What is less open to debate, regardless of Jesus' response, is that the narrator assumed that his followers carried weapons and at times felt free to use them (see also Lk. 22.36-38).

Two isolated incidents relating to the missionary activities of Paul and Simon Peter further support the claim that the disciples occasionally felt comfortable using physical violence. The first incident is contained in one of Paul's conversations with the Corinthians. In 1 Cor. 4.14–5.5 Paul expresses horror at the community's acceptance of a man who is having sexual relations with his father's wife, exclaiming: 'What would you prefer? Am I to come to you with a stick, or with love in a spirit of gentleness?' (4.21). Paul appears to be speaking figuratively here; nevertheless, his remark suggests a willingness to use corporal punishment if necessary. His remark shortly thereafter (5.4-5) is also relevant: 'When you are assembled, and my spirit is present with the power of our Lord Jesus, you are to hand this man over to Satan for the destruction of the flesh, so that his spirit may be saved in the day of the Lord.' It is not clear in this last quotation whether Paul is telling the Corinthians to have the man put to death or merely ostracized (in their view, exposing him more directly to the powers of Satan). Both sentences are harsh, but of course the first would be especially so. The second incident takes us back to the Ananias and Sapphira story recounted in Acts 5.1-11. What is striking in the Acts account is not only that God is thought to work through Simon Peter to kill Ananias (to make an example out of him, it would seem), but that Simon Peter allows it to happen again a few hours later to Ananias' wife Sapphira. If not the first time, at least the second, he becomes responsible for the murder of another human being, and Acts has him showing no hesitation or remorse. Both husband and wife have an extreme form of physical violence inflicted upon them for having lied. Even the ethic of 'an eye for an eye and a tooth for a tooth' seems to have been forgotten. Moreover, the story's intended deterrent force ('Be careful, fellow Christians: remember what happened when Ananias and Sapphira lied to Peter?') is a clear instance of psychological violence.

These are isolated incidents, as are the Gospel stories which show Jesus as content in using violence to achieve results. More frequent still are the references to God using violence to further his plans. A reading of the New Testament, then, leads to the impression that physical violence is sometimes acceptable. When these points are considered alongside the undercurrent of anger that runs through these texts, the violent image of the New Testament begins to emerge more distinctly from the *trompe l'oeil*.

3. *The Non-Pacifist Stance*

The above examples have shown that the New Testament sees nothing inherently wrong with the occasional use of physical violence on others if it serves an appropriate purpose. This section adds another component to that perspective: the New Testament also voices no objection to wars taking place, or to Christians serving in the military. Certain Christian churches (particularly the Brethren, Mennonites and Quakers) have long argued for pacifism and non-resistance based on their understanding of the New Testament. That understanding, however, is supported by a selective reading of the texts and by what is thought to be (whether rightly or wrongly) the 'essence' of the New Testament message. There are explicit examples to the contrary. This non-pacifist stance has implications for our study of violence, although they are ambiguous. A pacifist is not always peaceful or peace-promoting, and a soldier is not necessarily a 'warmonger'. The least that can be said is that the New Testament's open acceptance of soldiers and armies has continued to legitimate Christian participation in wars and violence.

Four passages provide a good overview of the New Testament attitude toward soldiers. The first two describe encounters of John the Baptist and Jesus with soldiers; the third presents a centurion's reaction to Jesus' death; and the fourth narrates in considerable detail the first conversion of a soldier to Christianity.

Soldiers appear early on in the Gospels. Luke mentions them coming to hear John (3.1-4):

> In the fifteenth year of the reign of Emperor Tiberius... the word of God came to John son of Zechariah in the wilderness. He went into all the region around the Jordan, proclaiming a baptism of repentance for the forgiveness of sins... John said to the crowds that came out to be baptized by him, 'You brood of vipers! Who warned you to flee from the wrath to come? Bear fruits worthy of repentance...' And the crowds asked him, 'What then should we do?' In reply he said to them, 'Whoever has two coats must share with anyone who has none; and whoever has food must do likewise.' Even tax collectors came to be baptized, and they asked him, 'Teacher, what should we do?' He said to them, 'Collect no more than the amount prescribed for you.' Soldiers also asked him, 'And we, what should we do?' He said to them, 'Do not extort money from anyone by threats or false accusation, and be satisfied with your wages.'

Luke's main point in this quotation is evident: John insists that a person's baptism 'of repentance for the forgiveness of sins' be followed by right living if it is to meet with God's acceptance. Living 'rightly' entails carrying out one's duties responsibly. Tax collectors are to be honest and soldiers are not to overstep their jurisdiction. Men are not criticized for being soldiers; instead, they are admonished to be good soldiers.

Jesus' example reinforces this point. The Gospels occasionally recount Jesus' interactions with non-Jews. The scenes are included to show that, although Jesus normally had nothing to do with these people, some of them evinced a faith strong enough to encourage him to meet their demands. His meeting with a Canaanite woman (Mt. 15.21-28; Mk 7.24-30) is a graphic example; his encounter with a centurion[12] is another (Lk. 7.1-10; see also Mt. 8.5-13):

> After Jesus had finished all his sayings in the hearing of the people, he entered Capernaum. A centurion there had a slave whom he valued highly, and who was ill and close to death. When he heard about Jesus, he sent some Jewish elders to him, asking him to come and heal his slave. When they came to Jesus, they appealed to him earnestly, saying, 'He is worthy of having you do this for him, for he loves our people, and it is he who built our synagogue for us.' And Jesus went with them, but when he was not far from the house, the centurion sent friends to say to him,

---

12. A centurion commanded one hundred men. The rank is roughly comparable to a captain.

'Lord, do not trouble yourself, for I am not worthy to have you come under my roof; therefore I did not presume to come to you. But only speak the word, and let my servant be healed. For I also am a man set under authority, with soldiers under me; and I say to one, "Go," and he goes, and to another, "Come," and he comes, and to my slave, "Do this," and the slave does it.' When Jesus heard this he was amazed at him, and turning to the crowd that followed him, he said, 'I tell you, not even in Israel have I found such faith.' When those who had been sent returned to the house, they found the slave in good health.

The Lukan Jesus is impressed by the centurion's unexpected show of faith. What surprises him is not that an army officer has shown such faith, but that the person with this extraordinary amount of faith is not Jewish. The man's occupation has absolutely nothing to do with Jesus' actions. In fact, the character of the centurion's military-based authority is compared to Jesus' authority. What matters is the man's faith in Jesus' healing powers—in this case, his great faith.

The next centurion to be impressed by Jesus stands at the foot of the cross and watches him die (Mk 15.39; see also Mt. 27.54 and Lk. 23.47): 'Now when the centurion, who stood facing him, saw that in this way he breathed his last, he said, "Truly this was God's Son!"' Luke's version (probably intended to make the centurion's statement more credible to his audience) has the centurion say instead: 'Certainly this man was innocent.' Again, nothing suggests that this confession of faith in Jesus is incompatible with the centurion's occupation. Rather, the point seems to be that even a centurion who was neither a Jew nor a Christian could experience the power of Jesus— and, as in the previous healing story, could evince the proper faith response. This message would have appealed to the early Christian communities, which were attracting an increasing proportion of their converts from outside the Jewish matrix.

The account in Acts of Cornelius's conversion, described at length in ch. 10, adds to these observations. Acts includes this incident in order to highlight the significance of the first non-Jewish conversion to Christianity. The story opens (10.1-8) with a description of Cornelius' uprightness and attraction to Judaism (as a 'God-fearer', meaning a person sympathetic to Judaism but not a convert):

In Caesarea there was a man named Cornelius, a centurion of the Italian Cohort, as it was called. He was a devout man who feared God with all his household; he gave alms generously to the people and prayed constantly to God. One afternoon at about three o'clock he had a vision in

which he clearly saw an angel of God coming in and saying to him,
'Cornelius.' He stared at him in terror and said, 'What is it, Lord?' He
answered, 'Your prayers and your alms have ascended as a memorial
before God. Now send men to Joppa for a certain Simon who is called
Peter; he is lodging with Simon, a tanner, whose house is by the seaside.'
When the angel who spoke to him had left, he called two of his slaves and
a devout soldier from the ranks of those who served him, and after telling
them everything, he sent them to Joppa.

Ignorant of this, Peter meanwhile is prepared for what is to occur by
receiving a vision of his own (10.9-16):

About noon the next day, as they were on their journey and approaching
the city, Peter went up on the roof to pray. He became hungry and wanted
something to eat; and while it was being prepared, he fell into a trance. He
saw the heaven opened and something like a large sheet coming down,
being lowered to the ground by its four corners. In it were all kinds of
fourfooted creatures and reptiles and birds of the air. Then he heard a
voice saying, 'Get up, Peter; kill and eat.' But Peter said, 'By no means,
Lord; for I have never eaten anything that is profane or unclean.' The
voice said to him again, a second time, 'What God has made clean, you
must not call profane.' This happened three times, and the thing was
suddenly taken up to heaven.

Puzzled by what he sees, Peter receives Cornelius' messengers and
makes his way with them to Caesarea (10.17-23). They arrive and are
greeted (10.24-29), and when Cornelius recounts his dream (10.30-33),
Peter responds (10.34-48):

'I truly understand that God shows no partiality, but in every nation
anyone who fears him and does what is right is acceptable to him.' While
Peter was still speaking, the Holy Spirit fell upon all who heard the word.
The circumcised believers who had come with Peter were astounded that
the gift of the Holy Spirit had been poured out even on the Gentiles, for
they heard them speaking in tongues and extolling God. Then Peter said,
'Can anyone withhold the water for baptizing these people who have
received the Holy Spirit just as we have?' So he ordered them to be baptized
in the name of Jesus Christ. Then they invited him to stay for several days.

This exchange is followed by Peter's need to convince the other
Christian leaders in Jerusalem of the legitimacy of this conversion.
The closing words to this narrative (11.17-18) are:

If then God gave them the same gift that he gave us when we believed in
the Lord Jesus Christ, who was I that I could hinder God? When they

> heard this, they were silenced. And they praised God, saying, 'Then God
> has given even to the Gentiles the repentance that leads to life.'

In each of these accounts there is no question of soldiers leaving
their profession to commit themselves to God. Being a soldier for
Rome is compatible with being a 'soldier for Christ'. Soldiers appear
in key scenes and show spiritual sensitivity. They are singled out as
one of the groups attracted to John the Baptist's preaching, and three
of them (centurions no less) in turn show great faith, great insight,
and great devotion. Moreover, according to Matthew and Mark a
centurion is the first human to appreciate Jesus' Sonship, and in Acts a
centurion is the first non-Jew worthy of becoming a Christian.

Not only are these soldiers not criticized for their choice of profession, they are exalted for their insights. The violent system of
which they are a part, and the violence they might have to inflict on
others, is also seen as compatible with their profession of faith, if it is
done by the rules. This stance suggests that the military metaphors so
loved by Paul are not his attempts to 'spiritualize' what he considered
unworthy of Christianity; rather, they reflect his recognition of the
importance and worth of the military—or at least his acceptance of it.[13]

So, the categorical 'No!' to human physical violence that is openly
stated (e.g., Mt. 26.52) and implied (e.g., Mt. 5.44) in several New
Testament passages must be qualified if one is searching for an all-
encompassing view of the New Testament. Violence is forbidden...but
it is acceptable if God or Jesus inflicts it, or, for that matter, if a
Christian leader does it occasionally. Violence is forbidden...but it is
acceptable if a Christian soldier inflicts it on others in the line of duty.

---

13. The first explicit reference to Christians serving in the Roman army is dated at
c. 175 CE during the reign of Marcus Aurelius (according to Eusebius, *Ecclesiastical
History* 5.5.1-7). Scholars dispute whether they served before this time. See Jean-
Michel Hornus, *It is Not Lawful for me to Fight: Early Christian Attitudes toward
War, Violence and the State* (trans. A. Kreider and O. Coburn; Scottsdale, PA:
Herald Press, 1980 [1960]); Adolph von Harnack, *Militia Christi: The Christian
Religion and the Military in the First Three Centuries* (trans. D. McInnes Gracie;
Philadelphia, PA: Fortress Press, 1981 [1905]); Cecil John Cadoux, *The Early
Christian Attitude to War: A Contribution to the History of Christian Ethics* (New
York, NY: Gordon Press, 1975 [1919]); and Peter Brock, *The Military Question in
the Early Church: A Selected Bibliography of a Century's Scholarship, 1888–1987*
(Toronto, ON: University of Toronto Press, 1990). A recent bibliographic overview
is David G. Hunter's 'A Decade of Research on Early Christians and Military
Service', in *Religious Studies Review* 18 (1992), pp. 87-94.

4. *The Apocalyptic World-View*

The earliest Christians, we have seen, lived in expectation of the imminent end of the world. On this matter they were not alone, for many Jewish literary works from this period attest to the same urgency. This eschatological issue is itself part of a larger 'apocalyptic' world view which evinced a preoccupation with all that would happen immediately before, during, and after the 'last days'. If the eschatological focus is difficult for many of us now to appreciate, its apocalyptic matrix presents us with even more problems. So I begin this section by sketching the parameters of that world view; then I turn to the image of God that undergirds it, and conclude by reflecting on apocalypticism's implications for the New Testament perspective on violence.

a. *The World-View*

Christians in the first century assumed that unseen spiritual forces were omnipresent. Some were controlled by God and others were not.[14] One could never be certain with which spiritual side one was dealing. At times, it was the divine forces that caused human suffering and natural disasters, while the 'satanic' forces provided rewards; other times it was the reverse. Both sides strived to control the earth (considered to be the heart of all creation). To do so they needed to control humans, who could be 'possessed' by both demons and God. Good and evil forces could manifest themselves to people in dreams, clothed in the bodies of humans or animals, or through natural events.

Understanding the workings of these spiritual forces was difficult enough in normal times, but the New Testament clearly shows that Christians in the first century considered themselves to be living in very special times. They believed that Jesus' presence on earth, combined with his death and resurrection, had dealt a serious blow to the forces of evil. Both sides now were on the verge of launching their final offensive. The world was about to enter particularly violent and traumatic times which would culminate in its total destruction. It was a 'winner take all' situation. Fortunately for Christians, the outcome

---

14. One finds no discussion from Christians during this time about how this situation arose. Is God responsible for evil? The gnostics in the mid-second century offer the first evidence of Christians addressing the topic. For an introduction to Gnosticism see K. Rudolph, *Gnosis: The Nature and History of Gnosticism* (trans. R. Mcl. Wilson; San Francisco: Harper and Row, 1983 [1975]).

of these battles had been 'revealed' (*apokalyptein*) to them in advance. So had the general framework of the struggle, yet much remained vague. These revelations informed them that the demonic forces would do their best to win humans to their side before the final confrontation with God occurred, and that most people would lack the power to resist. In addition, as cosmic terrorists of sorts, the evil forces would do their utmost to destabilize the world by inflicting unspeakable horrors on it. Finally, the divine forces would intervene, introducing a grand and cataclysmic battle in which evil would be utterly destroyed.

This description may sound like an extended metaphor for the human struggle against evil, but, as far as we can tell, most early Christians interpreted this understanding of reality quite literally. Many still do. They were deeply troubled not only by the horrors that awaited the world as they knew it but especially by the horrors that awaited them if their faith in God wavered ever so slightly. For after the final battle, Jesus would judge everyone, and those who had failed to live up to God's expectations would be punished mercilessly. They believed that, as Christians, they possessed special knowledge that made it easier for them to escape these punishments, but also that, as a consequence, more horrible punishments still awaited them if they were found wanting in their total commitment to God.

This apocalyptic world view, then, was overtly violent: Satan and his forces were determined to inflict horrific violence on earth and on humankind, and in this respect God was no different. Christians might speak of having 'peace with God' now and hopefully after the final battle, and they might exhort one another to 'live peaceably' in the meantime, but superimposed on these sanctuaries of 'peace' was an awesomely violent context.

b. *The Image of God*
Many twentieth-century Christians believe that the vengeful, wrathful God who leads his people into war is not 'their God', but the 'God of the Old Testament'. This God certainly can be found striding through the pages of the Hebrew Bible (the Christian 'Old Testament'), but he is also to be found in the New Testament, leading his people into war and imposing his wrath on their enemies. The New Testament occasionally even acknowledges that the God who helped his people win battles in biblical times is also their God (e.g., Acts 7.45; 13.19; Heb. 11.32-34).

The New Testament God makes war mainly in the end times. One symbolic depiction of this activity is in Revelation 19.11–20.3:

> Then I saw heaven opened, and there was a white horse! Its rider is called Faithful and True, and in righteousness he judges and makes war. His eyes are like a flame of fire, and on his head are many diadems; and he has a name inscribed that no one knows but himself. He is clothed in a robe dipped in blood, and his name is called The Word of God. And the armies of heaven, wearing fine linen, white and pure, were following him on white horses. From his mouth comes a sharp sword with which to strike down the nations, and he will rule them with a rod of iron; he will tread the winepress of the fury of the wrath of God the Almighty. On his robe and on his thigh he has a name inscribed, 'King of kings and Lord of lords.'
>
> Then I saw an angel standing in the sun, and with a loud voice he called to all the birds that fly in midheaven, 'Come, gather for the great supper of God, to eat the flesh of kings, the flesh of captains, the flesh of the mighty, the flesh of horses and their riders—flesh of all, both free and slave, both small and great.' Then I saw the beast and the kings of the earth with their armies gathered to make war against the rider on the horse and against his army. And the beast was captured, and with it the false prophet who had performed in its presence the sign by which he deceived those who had received the mark of the beast and those who worshipped its image. These two were thrown alive into the lake of fire that burns with sulphur. And the rest were killed by the sword of the rider on the horse, the sword that came from his mouth; and all the birds were gorged with their flesh. Then I saw an angel coming down from heaven, holding in his hand the key to the bottomless pit and a great chain. He seized the dragon, that ancient serpent, who is the Devil and Satan, and bound him for a thousand years, and threw him into the pit, and locked and sealed it over him, so that he would deceive the nations no more, until the thousand years were ended. After that he must be let out for a little while.

To what extent the early Christians assumed that this war would include Christian participation is unclear; that there would be human victims, though, is certain. The New Testament descriptions of the events leading up to the end time (e.g., 2 Thess. 2; Mk 13), however, do include spiritually induced wars and other events in which human involvement is expected. An example is found in Mt. 24.1-8:

> As Jesus came out of the temple and was going away, his disciples came to point out to him the buildings of the temple. Then he asked them, 'You see all these, do you not? Truly I tell you, not one stone will be left here upon another; all will be thrown down.' When he was sitting on the Mount of Olives, the disciples came to him privately, saying, 'Tell us,

> when will this be, and what will be the sign of your coming and the end
> of the age?' Jesus answered them, 'Beware that no one leads you astray.
> For many will come in my name, saying, "I am the Messiah!" and they
> will lead many astray. And you will hear rumors of wars; see that you are
> not alarmed; for this must take place, but the end is not yet. For nation
> will rise against nation, and kingdom against kingdom, and there will be
> famines and earthquakes in various places: all this is but the beginning of
> the birthpangs.'

It is also clear that God's acts of violence are not restricted to the
very end times. We have seen how Acts has him working through
Peter to kill Ananias and Sapphira. Matthew's Parable of the Wedding
Banquet makes the same point. This is an allegorized form of a
parable which also occurs in Lk. 14.16-24. The components are easily
discerned: the king stands for God, the two groups of slaves are the
prophets of the Hebrew Bible and some of Jesus' disciples, the city
that is destroyed is Jerusalem in 70 CE, and the people brought in
from the streets are the non-Jews (Mt. 22.2-10):

> The kingdom of heaven may be compared to a king who gave a wedding
> banquet for his son. He sent his slaves to call those who had been invited
> to the wedding banquet, but they would not come. Again he sent other
> slaves, saying, 'Tell those who have been invited: Look, I have prepared
> my dinner, my oxen and my fat calves have been slaughtered, and every-
> thing is ready; come to the wedding banquet.' But they made light of it
> and went away, one to his farm, another to his business, while the rest
> seized his slaves, mistreated them, and killed them. The king was
> enraged. He sent his troops, destroyed those murderers, and burned their
> city. Then he said to his slaves, 'The wedding is ready, but those invited
> were not worthy. Go therefore into the main streets, and invite everyone
> you find to the wedding banquet.' Those slaves went out into the streets
> and gathered all whom they found, both good and bad; so the wedding
> hall was filled with guests.

This parable reinforces the Judaeo-Christian perspective of a God who
continually intervenes in wars. He controls history and occasionally
acts decisively in order to redirect it.

Outside the book of Revelation, the New Testament has few
extended passages which concentrate on the divine battles. The focus
instead lies on the coming wrath of God upon unbelievers. The end of
the Matthean parable quoted above (22.11-14) suggests what will
happen even to Christians who are not fully prepared (who lack a
'wedding robe'):

> But when the king came in to see the guests, he noticed a man there who was not wearing a wedding robe, and he said to him, 'Friend, how did you get in here without a wedding robe?' And he was speechless. Then the king said to the attendants, 'Bind him hand and foot, and throw him into the outer darkness, where there will be weeping and gnashing of teeth.' For many are called, but few are chosen.

For his part, the author of Hebrews insists that 'God is a consuming fire' (12.29) and reminds his audience (10.26-31):

> For if we willfully persist in sin after having received the knowledge of the truth, there no longer remains a sacrifice for sins, but a fearful prospect of judgment, and a fury of fire that will consume the adversaries. Anyone who has violated the law of Moses dies without mercy 'on the testimony of two or three witnesses.' How much worse punishments do you think will be deserved by those who have spurned the Son of God, profaned the blood of the covenant by which they were sanctified, and outraged the Spirit of grace? For we know the one who said, 'Vengeance is mine, I will repay.' And again, 'The Lord will judge his people.' It is a fearful thing to fall into the hands of the living God.

Paul also speaks frequently about the wrath of God. Only Jesus can save humans from this wrath, he claims (Rom. 9.5). Eleven of those references to God's wrath occur in Romans (1.18; 2.5, 8; 3.5; 4.15; 5.19; 9.22, 22; 12.19; 13.4, 5). A passage from 2 Thessalonians (1.6-10) graphically describes this view:

> For it is indeed just of God to repay with affliction those who afflict you, and to give relief to the afflicted as well as to us, when the Lord Jesus is revealed from heaven with his mighty angels in flaming fire, inflicting vengeance on those who do not know God and on those who do not obey the gospel of our Lord Jesus. These will suffer the punishment of eternal destruction, separated from the presence of the Lord and from the glory of his might, when he comes to be glorified by his saints and to be marveled at on that day among all who have believed, because our testimony to you was believed.

This wrath is also mirrored in an exorcism described by Mark (5.1-13), which symbolically points, among other things, to the coming destruction of the Roman troops. The man in the story below, whose demon answers to the name 'legion', symbolizes the occupation of the Jewish people and their land by a Roman legion. The narrative resolution, in which the legion is sent into the lake like swine, would have delighted the audience, fulfilling the Jews' wish to triumph over and denigrate the Roman occupying force. Jesus' powers of exorcism anticipate the wrath of God that will soon descend on the Romans.[15]

> They came to the other side of the sea, to the country of the Gerasenes. And when he had stepped out of the boat, immediately a man out of the tombs with an unclean spirit met him. He lived among the tombs; and no one could restrain him any more, even with a chain; for he had often been restrained with shackles and chains, but the chains he wrenched apart, and the shackles he broke in pieces; and no one had the strength to subdue him. Night and day among the tombs and on the mountains he was always howling and bruising himself with stones. When he saw Jesus from a distance, he ran and bowed down before him; and he shouted at the top of his voice, 'What have you to do with me, Jesus, Son of the Most High God? I adjure you by God, do not torment me.' For he had said to him, 'Come out of the man, you unclean spirit!' Then Jesus asked him, 'What is your name?' He replied, 'My name is Legion; for we are many.' He begged him earnestly not to send them out of the country. Now there on the hillside a great herd of swine was feeding; and the unclean spirits begged him, 'Send us into the swine; let us enter them.' So he gave them permission. And the unclean spirits came out and entered the swine; and the herd, numbering about two thousand, rushed down the steep bank into the sea, and were drowned in the sea.

Jesus is also said to pronounce an oracle of judgment upon cities that do not welcome his disciples (Lk. 10.13-16):

> Woe to you, Chorazin! Woe to you, Bethsaida! For if the deeds of power done in you had been done in Tyre and Sidon, they would have repented long ago, sitting in sackcloth and ashes. But at the judgment it will be more tolerable for Tyre and Sidon than for you. And you, Capernaum, will you be exalted to heaven? No, you will be brought down to Hades. Whoever listens to you listens to me, and whoever rejects you rejects me, and whoever rejects me rejects the one who sent me.

The book of Revelation is not silent on this topic. Its author believes that God and his helpers (e.g. Jesus in 19.11) will reward those whose names are written 'in the book of life' (13.8), since they have acted faithfully (20.12-13) and given him glory (16.9), and will inflict horrific punishment on the others (e.g. 9.20-21; 6.16-17). Indeed, even before the final judgment the punishments will be gruesome (15.5–16.20):

15. The evangelists probably intend to make the same point in narrating the story of Jesus overturning tables in the temple. This image functions well as a symbol for what God is expected to do in the end time.

After this I looked, and the temple of the tent of witness in heaven was opened, and out of the temple came the seven angels with the seven plagues, robed in pure bright linen, with golden sashes across their chests. Then one of the four living creatures gave the seven angels seven golden bowls full of the wrath of God, who lives forever and ever; and the temple was filled with smoke from the glory of God and from his power, and no one could enter the temple until the seven plagues of the seven angels were ended. Then I heard a loud voice from the temple telling the seven angels, 'Go and pour out on the earth the seven bowls of the wrath of God.' So the first angel went and poured his bowl on the earth, and a foul and painful sore came on those who had the mark of the beast and who worshipped the image. The second angel poured his bowl into the sea, and it became like the blood of a corpse, and every living thing in the sea died. The third angel poured his bowl into the rivers and the springs of water, and they became blood. And I heard the angel of the waters say, 'You are just, O Holy One, who are and were, for you have judged these things; because they shed the blood of saints and prophets, you have given them blood to drink. It is what they deserve!' And I heard the altar respond, 'Yes, O Lord God, the Almighty, your judgments are true and just!'

The fourth angel poured his bowl on the sun, and it was allowed to scorch them with fire; they were scorched by the fierce heat, but they cursed the name of God, who had authority over these plagues, and they did not repent and give him glory. The fifth angel poured his bowl on the throne of the beast, and its kingdom was plunged into darkness; people gnawed their tongues in agony, and cursed the God of heaven because of their pains and sores, and they did not repent of their deeds. The sixth angel poured his bowl on the great river Euphrates, and its water was dried up in order to prepare the way for the kings from the east. And I saw three foul spirits like frogs coming from the mouth of the dragon, from the mouth of the beast, and from the mouth of the false prophet. These are demoniac spirits, performing signs, who go abroad to the kings of the whole world, to assemble them for battle on the great day of God the Almighty... And they assembled them at the place that in Hebrew is called Harmagedon.

The seventh angel poured his bowl onto the air, and a loud voice came out of the temple, from the throne, saying, 'It is done!' And there came flashes of lightning, rumblings, peals of thunder, and a violent earthquake, such as had not occurred since people were upon the earth, so violent was that earthquake. The great city was split into three parts, and the cities of the nations fell. God remembered great Babylon and gave her the wine-cup of the fury of his wrath. And every island fled away, and no mountains were to be found; and huge hailstones, each weighing about a hundred pounds, dropped from heaven on people, until they cursed God for the plague of hail, so fearful was that plague.

The God of the New Testament is not a 'nice God'. In addition to his role as father and comforter, he is depicted as warrior, judge, vindicator and avenger. Furthermore, as Paul's remarks to the Corinthians remind us, at times Jesus takes God's place: 'For all of us must appear before the judgment seat of Christ, so that each may receive recompense for what has been done in the body, whether good or evil' (2 Cor. 5.10). We have here a distinct mix: the New Testament texts speak of non-retaliation and love of enemies when it comes to human conduct, but this is understood in the context of divine violence and vengeance.[16]

c. *The Implications*
The New Testament apocalyptic perspective, in particular its portrayal of God and Jesus as wrathful warriors, leads to the devaluation of the present world and a division of humanity into groups of 'saved' and 'damned'. If the world is about to end, there is not much sense in preserving or reforming it, and on the whole the New Testament writings show very little interest in such matters. 'Our citizenship is in heaven', Paul says to the Philippians (3.20). Suggesting constructive ways to resolve inequities between the rich and the poor, or slaves and their masters, matters little to the writers of the New Testament. The result is their acceptance of what is now called 'structural violence', whereby the inequalities and injustices built into the political and religious institutions are allowed to stand.[17] Moreover, the differentiation of humanity into two groups facilitates the stereotyping of enemies ('the devil's brood' in John's Gospel, 'heathen' and 'pagans' in subsequent centuries), thus denying all people their full equality. Certainly the apocalyptic model does not project a new order in which all people are to achieve personal dignity and autonomy. Personal and structural violence, which are both part of the apocalyptic world view, create difficulties for people who are intent on working for a peaceful future.

16. William Klassen argues that the God of the Bible is not vengeful; rather, God occasionally merely asserts his 'imperium' or 'sovereignty'. This distinction, it seems to me, makes sense, but only if one begins the examination with the presupposition that God is 'good' and 'just'. See *Love of Enemies: The Way to Peace* (Philadelphia, PA: Fortress Press, 1984), pp. 43-47.

17. A remark by Martin Luther King, Jr reinforces this point: 'What is so disturbing is not the appalling actions of the "bad" people, but the appalling silence of the "good" people.' Quoted by Brown, *Religion and Violence*, p. 55.

Another type of violence emerges from the problem-solving model promoted by this stance. Everything is ultimately in God's hands: God creates and destroys, God fights the battles and punishes his opponents. Concerning the larger problems besetting the world, humans sit back and wait for God's intervention. In the process they have little autonomy, control, or personal dignity, except insofar as it comes to doing what they can to protect themselves from evil. More important, in the end violence decides matters. The stronger force wins. God the father will handle matters for people.

There are positive corollaries to God taking care of all the 'dirty work'. For some people this transfer of violence and anger onto a God figure helps to remove it safely from this world and this time. From a socio-political perspective, containing and redirecting one's frustrations can be better than allowing them to tumble directly into the community.

For others, however, this apocalyptic view of God spills over directly into their lives. Simply put: since God is our model and he solves his problems through violence, so can we. A modern analogy might be helpful in drawing out some of the implications. Pornography, which often includes scenes of violence directed at women and children, is often excused on the grounds that it is a harmless, violence-redirecting fantasy for some males who might otherwise be engaging in physical acts of violence against women and children. Yet pornography in fact contributes continuously to the degradation of women—itself a serious form of violence—and it occasionally leads to actual physical violence against women. Pornography does not only—or even—serve as a harmless outlet for male fantasies. The same can be said about the image of an aggressive and violent God that is projected onto the pages of the New Testament.

The apocalyptic scenario, therefore, so graphically reinforced throughout the New Testament, not only depicts in abstraction a violent God. It has implications on how the readers of the New Testament lead their lives. This world view is not particularly helpful in promoting a lasting peace, if such a peace presupposes the equal worth of each individual and the intention to build a better world with opportunities for everyone. Apocalypticism shows no interest in these issues. In fact, it works against them. For this reason—not so much the graphic scenes of violence which one finds in the strictly apocalyptic passages—one could argue that the apocalyptic stance, so important in the New Testament, is fundamentally violent in nature.

5. *The Role of Women*

The New Testament does not encourage the physical abuse of women; nevertheless, a great deal of violence is directed against them in this corpus, since violence includes more than physical acts of aggression. Rape, for instance, is an overt expression of physical violence against women, but societal factors that allow rape to occur promote this physical violence and can themselves be considered violent.

Before discussing the violence directed at women, I begin this section by describing elements of the peace-promoting portrayal of women in the New Testament. This could have been covered in the previous chapter; I include it here in order to highlight the non-physical component of this violence.

a. *The Peace-promoting Portrayals*

Paul's categorical statement in Gal. 3.28 ('There is no longer Jew or Greek, there is no longer slave or free, there is no longer male and female') on the whole is supported by his remarks about women throughout his letters. In 1 Cor. 7.2-5, for instance, Paul reminds his community that within marriage both husband and wife are to respect each other's sexual desires. What applies to men also applies to women:

> But because of cases of sexual immorality, each man should have his own wife and each woman her own husband. The husband should give to his wife her conjugal rights, and likewise the wife to her husband. For the wife does not have authority over her own body, but the husband does; likewise the husband does not have authority over his own body, but the wife does. Do not deprive one another except perhaps by agreement for a set time, to devote yourselves to prayer, and then come together again, so that Satan may not tempt you because of your lack of self-control.

This egalitarian stance is not unusual in Paul's letters. Throughout his churches women appear to have been as involved as men in most aspects of religious life. His extended greetings in the last chapter of Romans give a good impression of this stance. Paul begins by mentioning Phoebe (16.1-2):

> I commend to you our sister Phoebe; a deacon of the church at Cenchreae, so that you may welcome her in the Lord as is fitting for the saints, and

help her in whatever she may require from you, for she has been a bene-
factor of many and of myself as well.

He then moves on to the wife and husband team of Prisca and Aquila
(16.3-5): 'Greet Prisca and Aquila, who work with me in Christ Jesus,
and who risked their necks for my life, to whom not only I give
thanks, but also all the churches of the Gentiles. Greet also the church
in their house.' Paul continues to name both men and women who
have been involved in his churches.[18] One of these greetings is
perhaps more important than the others: 'Greet Andronicus and Junia,
my relatives who were in prison with me; they are prominent among
the apostles, and they were in Christ before I was' (16.7). 'Junia' (or
'Junias') is either a man or a woman; the Greek text cannot help us to
decide. What makes the issue important is that if the person is a
woman, Paul provides the only New Testament evidence for a woman
having the status of an apostle. Regardless, Paul's overall presentation
of women, as respected church members who were actively engaged
with men in Christian missionary work, remains vivid.

A similar picture emerges from the Gospels' presentation of women
in Jesus' public activities. Women may not figure as prominently as
men in the Gospels, but they nevertheless play important roles. For
instance, Lk. 8.3 suggests that some women funded Jesus' religious
campaign. According to Mark, after Jesus' abandonment by his
disciples, only the women remain faithful until the end. They appear
at the crucifixion (15.40-41), the burial (15.47), and the discovery of
the empty tomb (16.1-8). John's Gospel is particularly striking in this
regard. This evangelist wants his audience to understand that women
played an important role in Jesus' life. At times he does this by having
the disciples play the foil. For instance, at the end of Jesus' long,
private dialogue with the Samaritan woman, the disciples return and
all they can do is marvel that their master 'was talking with a woman'
(4.27). John also effectively transmits this impression by sprinkling
his narrative with strong female characters: Mary, mother of Jesus
(2.11; 19.25-27), the Samaritan woman (4.7-42), Mary and Martha of
Bethany (11.1–12.8), and Mary Magdalene (19.25–20.18). Jesus'
mother instigates his first miracle, at Cana; the Samaritan woman is
given the honour of being the first to convert her people; Martha's

18. For insight on the importance of women in Romans 16 see Richardson,
'From Apostles to Virgins'.

understanding of Jesus in 11.27 captures his importance as well as anyone else in this Gospel; and to Mary Magdalene goes the privilege of being the first to see the risen Jesus.

The Johannine portrayal of women is more pointed and positive than one finds in the other Gospels, but it still is consistent with the overall New Testament view that women played active and respected roles in Christian community life in Jesus' day and shortly afterwards. This is remarkable, given the first and second-century context of the New Testament documents. We lack the historical data with which to be certain about the precise place of women in the Jewish and Greco-Roman societies of that day, but we know enough to say that on the whole early Christian communities offered women at least as much freedom and equality as they would have had in other contemporary groups, and more than most.[19]

From a historical perspective, we should expect no more from a collection of first-century documents—especially when one considers that their selection in a sacred canon was finalized centuries later, at a time when the patriarchalization of this religion had become firmly entrenched. But this is not just any collection of first-century documents. The New Testament continues to exert considerable influence on our society, and we need to judge it also by our standards. When we do so on this issue of sexual equality, it does not stand up well.[20] What follows is a description of how the New Testament model of women, however respectable it may have been in the first century, is not consistent with the twentieth-century Euro-North American ideal, which is based on the principle that men and women should be considered equal in every respect.

19. For additional information see Leonard Swidler, *Women in Judaism: The Status of Women in Formative Judaism* (Metuchen, NJ: Scarecrow Press, 1976); Bernadette Brooten, *Women Leaders in the Ancient Synagogue: Inscriptional Evidence and Background* (Chico, CA: Scholars Press, 1982); and Sarah Pomeroy, *Goddesses, Whores, Wives, and Slaves: Women in Classical Antiquity* (New York, NY: Schocken Books, 1975).

20. People react to this fact differently. Some use it as a reason to discard the twentieth-century ideal of equality; conversely, others use it to discard Christianity. The tendency among Christian scholars is to seek an egalitarian 'core' to the New Testament upon which to build their faith—e.g., in the reconstructed teachings of Jesus, the 'authentic' Paul.

b. *The Violence*

All the New Testament writers are men.[21] This fact goes a long way toward explaining why, with few exceptions (e.g., Jn 4.1-38; 11.1-44; 12.1-8), the scenes are all presented from a male perspective, with male protagonists, and with male preoccupations. Family matters, the raising of children, cooking and cleaning—all important traditional female concerns—are never discussed directly. One need only compare this with the energy expended by Paul on whether 'Christians' ought to be circumcised or not.

The 'antitheses' in Matthew's Sermon on the Mount, which certainly can appear to have strong peace-promoting characteristics, as we have seen in the previous chapter, are also fundamentally androcentric. It would be an overstatement to say that Jesus, in these exhortations, excludes women, but it is fair to say that he is speaking as a man to other men. The first antithesis, for instance (5.21-26), is concerned explicitly with reconciliation between male Christians (each person is called an *adelphos*, or brother, in Greek). The second (5.27-30) and especially the third (5.31-32—Jewish women were not allowed to divorce their husbands) also have a male audience in mind:

> But I say to you that everyone who looks at a woman with lust has already committed adultery with her in his heart... [and] anyone who divorces his wife, except on the ground of unchastity, causes her to commit adultery.

The same can be said for the fifth antithesis and its famous 'turn the other cheek' exhortation. This pacifist advice, given in a context in which the oppressor expects the victim to strike back, accords well with male aggressive tendencies.[22] Expecting a beaten male to 'turn the other cheek' may he extraordinary; expecting the same of a

21. This claim is traditional, and almost certainly correct, but it cannot be proven. In fact, we are not certain who wrote most of the New Testament books. In the face of this uncertainty, claims have been made for the female authorship of John's Gospel (e.g., by E. Schüssler-Fiorenza, *In Memory of her* [New York, NY: Crossroad, 1983]), but there is very little supporting textual evidence for this position.

22. I owe this insight concerning the androcentrism of the 'turn the other cheek' injunction to Luise Schottroff, in an oral presentation she made at the University of Toronto, 10 May, 1991. She noted that a woman's natural instinct, when battered, is less likely to be direct physical retaliation. Not all women, to be sure, would fit this characterization (the same can be said for the reverse position concerning men), but Schottroff's point is still valuable.

woman is not as remarkable, but Jesus' extraordinarily remarkable antitheses were not directed to female Christians.

In spite of the occasional prominence of a few women throughout the New Testament, the great majority remain invisible: their presence in the New Testament narratives is easily forgotten. Not many of Jesus' male followers are featured in the New Testament narratives either, but in comparison to women they still dominate. The story about Jesus feeding the 'five thousand' is instructive in this regard. All four Gospels indicate that he fed five thousand men.[23] Mark (6.44), Luke (9.14) and John (6.10) leave it at that; only Matthew (14.21) mentions in passing that the women and children were there as well. In the public arena women could literally not count. The case of Peter's missing wife is another example. The Synoptic Gospels recount Jesus' healing of Simon Peter's mother-in-law (Mk 1.29-31; Mt. 8.14-15; Lk. 4.38-39). To the attentive reader this story raises the unanswered question of whether Peter's wife was still alive. Paul in 1 Cor. 9.5 fortunately provides more information on this matter, but quite by chance. In this passage, Paul insists that he refuses to get paid for his services—nor does he travel with a wife, 'as do the other apostles and the brothers of the Lord and Cephas [Peter]'. This tells us that the Christian leaders may have often travelled with their wives.[24] But if it were not for Paul's offhand remark, which is aimed at defending his own practice, we would have never guessed that the apostles' wives travelled with them, or even that the apostles had wives! Acts tells us how many converts were won over to Christianity, but it does not tell us who cooked their meals. This curious imbalance partly reflects the fact that the image of Jesus and the development of the early churches come to us exclusively through the eyes of the men who wrote the accounts.

23. Greek distinguishes between 'man' (*aner*) and 'person' (*anthropos*), and in this story all four writers say 'men'. Almost all English versions make it difficult to appreciate the force of 'men' here because elsewhere they translate both *aner* and *anthropos* as 'man'. The New Revised Standard Version (used in this study) avoids using 'man' and 'mankind' for *anthropos*.

24. It may also tell us that Paul himself was married, but we cannot be certain. All that we can conclude from his letters (notably 1 Cor. 7) is that if he was (still) married he was not having sexual intercourse with his wife. The fact that his married status (and Jesus', for that matter) can remain in doubt supports the point that the wives of the early Christians were not considered important by the writers of the New Testament.

The main characters in the New Testament books are also exclusively male. The twelve close followers chosen by Jesus are men, as are the principal church leaders (Peter, Paul, Barnabas, etc.) and their successors (Timothy, Titus, etc.). From the outset this has promoted the belief that men are the rightful leaders in the churches.[25] God and Jesus, of course, are also considered male. In a first-century Jewish context, this would have raised no eyebrows; in a Greco-Roman context, where both male and female gods were commonplace, the maleness of the Christian divinity would have appeared more restrictive than it does to us. Centuries of exposure to the Judaeo-Christian-Muslim model of God have desensitized many of us to female models of divinity and the extreme maleness of the Christian model.[26]

Not only are the characters all male, but they tend to assume what some now call 'male' roles: they make the decisions; they know what is best for their communities. Jesus, for instance, often attempts to solve problems through confrontation and violence rather than dialogue and compromise. John's Gospel is the most blatant example of this behaviour; throughout this narrative Jesus at best is insulting to outsiders. For the women and men who do not understand leadership in this manner, the New Testament is not particularly helpful.

We might call this a mild form of violence exhibited against women and wonder whether perhaps it reflects a New Testament view that women ought to be subordinate to men. What makes the situation more serious, though, is that women not only tend to be ignored and presented with role models with which they can relate only with difficulty, but in several New Testament texts they are also explicitly considered inferior by nature to men. Two passages in one of Paul's letters to the Corinthians are important in this regard. The first occurs in his exhortation to the community concerning ritual practices during prayer and worship. His point is plain: women should cover their heads and men should not. His argument is more difficult to trace. Scripture supports this view, he insists (11.3-10); so does nature

25. In 1977 Pope Paul VI declared that a woman cannot be a priest in the Catholic Church 'because our Lord was a man' (quoted by Elaine Pagels in *The Gnostic Gospels* [New York, NY: Random House, 1979], p. 69).

26. In this context, the Acts account of Paul's God replacing Artemis in Asia (19.23-27) is particularly revealing. With modern eyes, sensitized to a feminist critique of patriarchal traditions, this story emerges as a narration of the triumph of the male Jewish god over the Asian mother goddess.

(11.13-15) and church practice (11.16). The tone is roughly as follows. Do what I say because I have the backing of God…and if that is not enough, look around you, and you will see that it is simply common sense…and if that still does not convince you, do it anyway because that is the Christian way: 'But if anyone is disposed to be contentious—we have no such custom, nor do the churches of God' (11.16). The defensive nature of the presentation suggests that Paul is arriving at some compromise with his group (or perhaps that he has changed his mind). Imbedded in the discussion about Scripture is the statement: 'But I want you to understand that Christ is the head of every man, and the husband is the head of his wife, and God is the head of Christ' (11.3). With this remark, Paul reveals that he has in mind a hierarchical order, which goes back to creation and places women under men (11.7-9):

> For a man ought not to have his head veiled, since he is the image and reflection of God; but woman is the reflection of man. Indeed, man was not made from woman, but woman from man. Neither was man created for the sake of woman, but woman for the sake of man.

This reasoning carries over into 14.34-36, where Paul in exasperation lashes out at the female members of that community:

> As in all the churches of the saints, women should be silent in the churches. For they are not permitted to speak, but should be subordinate, as the law also says. If there is anything they desire to know, let them ask their husbands at home. For it is shameful for a woman to speak in church. Or did the word of God originate with you?

The context of this remark (chs. 12–14) suggests that women have shown particular proficiency in speaking in tongues, causing disturbances and confusion in his church. Paul wants the Corinthian community to downplay this 'gift'. His outburst, though, still highlights his basic understanding of the women's place. This attitude is probably founded on a literal reading of Gen. 3.16, a verse conveying the result of the 'fall': 'To the woman he said, "I will greatly increase your pangs in childbearing; in pain you shall bring forth children, yet your desire shall be for your husband, and he shall rule over you."'

Ephesians (5.21-33), Colossians (3.18-25) and Titus (2.2-5) reinforce what the writers perceive to be a healthy married lifestyle, and in so doing they also reinforce this biblically-grounded subjugation of women. Colossians states: 'Wives, be subject to your husbands, as is fitting in the Lord' (Col. 3.18). Eph. 5.23 adds: 'For the husband is the head of the wife just as Christ is the head of the church, the body of which is the Saviour.' And Tit. 2.5 presents what would become the standard Christian model for women: they are to 'be self-controlled, chaste, good managers of the household, kind, being submissive to their husbands'. A passage from 1 Tim. 2.9-15 can serve as a summary for these texts:

> The women should dress themselves modestly and decently in suitable clothing, not with their hair braided, or with gold, pearls, or expensive clothes, but with good works, as is proper for women who profess reverence for God. Let a woman learn in silence with full submission. I permit no woman to teach or to have authority over a man; she is to keep silent. For Adam was formed first, then Eve; and Adam was not deceived, but the woman was deceived and became a transgressor. Yet she will be saved through childbearing, provided they continue in faith and love and holiness, with modesty.

A woman's role, according to these New Testament letters, is to raise children and show proper submission to her husband. Through this she earns her salvation. Two scriptural texts from the creation stories are used to support the author's position that women are naturally inferior: Adam was made first (Gen. 2.7), which makes him superior; and it was Eve who was deceived by the serpent (Gen. 3.6), which makes her weaker. It matters little that these scriptural supports themselves are weak and selective (e.g., according to the first creation story, in Genesis 1, man and woman were created together, and according to Genesis 3 both husband and wife eat of the forbidden fruit). What matters is that they were considered strong enough in Paul's day and afterwards to support the community standard. On this matter the New Testament speaks strongly. Women may join the community and participate on several levels, but not fully as equals. By nature they are inferior to men, and to this view Scripture gives its divine seal of approval.

If violence—to refer again to Robert McAfee Brown's definition—is the 'violation of personhood', the New Testament denial of full equality to women is essentially violent. As a result, one can decry the institutional violence against women that has resulted from this New Testament viewpoint: many churches today still do not allow women to be religious leaders, a fact that has also slowed egalitarian reforms throughout our entire society. One can also suggest that this viewpoint has made it easier for Christian men to justify their physical domination of women over the centuries. These views are based on the principle that to deny women full equality is to participate in violence. Beneath the New Testament veneer of equality lies a great deal of this violence.

6. *The Insider–Outsider Mentality*

The violence-inducing attitude which comes from considering one part of humanity superior to the other carries over to the missionary arena. Each New Testament writer insists that there is only one way to gain God's favour: his way. No dissent is allowed from Christians who might have different interpretations of that way, and no compromise is possible with non-Christians. Moreover, as we have seen, these writers presume that the world is dominated by the forces of evil and the forces of good, and that people are controlled by one side or the other. Consequently, dissidents and outsiders are considered not only wrong but controlled by evil—and, if nothing changes, they will also be punished severely and damned. There is no middle ground. There is little respect for other possibilities of appreciating God or humanity. The New Testament 'we–they' perspective is developed on the one hand by setting others apart, and on the other by reinforcing the sense of belonging.[27] This tendency is not surprising. Sociologists have shown how groups must create boundaries if they are to survive. Paul creates boundaries particularly well by emphasizing, in letters to his communities, the advantages of being an insider and the liabilities of being an outsider.

This perspective is not accompanied by an exhortation to inflict physical violence on the 'outsider'. While it does happen occasionally, almost always the New Testament portrays Christians as innocent in this regard. They know they are right and righteous in God's eyes, and they believe that those who oppose them or ignore them will soon have violence inflicted on them by Jesus and God unless they convert.

27. Robert Jewett (*The Captain America Complex: The Dilemma of Zealous Nationalism* [Santa Fe, NM: Bear and Company, 2nd edn, 1984]) calls this the 'Good Guys vs. Bad Guys Syndrome', and argues that American politics has often taken its inspiration from this New Testament model. More recently, Burton Mack forcefully makes the same point in *A Myth of Innocence: Mark and Christian Origins* (Philadelphia, PA: Fortress Press, 1988), especially pp. 351-76.

But they themselves have no blood on their hands. Yet the violence still remains. By this I do not mean the killing of millions of 'outsiders' over the centuries by Christians who modelled themselves on God. I mean a lack of respect for another person's right to exist and be different. To insist that all those who refuse the 'good news about Christ' are inherently lesser, evil, damnable individuals is to inflict violence on them. This section outlines the extent to which that belief is manifested in the New Testament. I will not explore the profound social and psychological implications that derive from relegating most of humanity to the category of 'outsider'.

The Gospels, as we now appreciate with more anguish than our predecessors, have a strong anti-Judaic tone. Recent attempts by well-meaning Christians to present it differently do not do justice to the textual evidence. The Jews in the New Testament, with varying degrees of intensity and passion, are treated as outsiders who resist Jesus and who play an important role in his arrest and death. This presentation of the Jews poignantly reveals the two basic strata of the Jesus story embedded in the Gospels. The primary stratum is the simple story of Jesus, considered by his followers to be the Son of God, having his status questioned by the Jews and being put to death at the instigation of his own people. On this level (and from a Christian perspective), the Jewish leaders and many of the Jewish people are seen as ignorant at best and villainous at worst. Judas is a traitor who deserves to die. Indeed, Jesus' death would only serve to reinforce the frustration and anger felt by his followers. The other stratum is secondary. It is based on the reinterpretation of Jesus which took place after his death, when his followers came to believe that his death had been part of God's plan, and had been predicted in the Scriptures. It was needed to 'cleanse' the world and to serve notice that evil was about to be destroyed utterly. On this level, the Jews who resisted Jesus' message, and Judas who 'betrayed' him, become, if not heroes perhaps, at least God's agents who played important parts in saving all of humanity. Jews should be presented as anguished pawns in the divine plan for salvation. But they are not. Level two sets the parameters for the Gospels' narrative presentations, but level one continues to set the tone. In a story about the divinely ordained death of Jesus, the Jews who helped to put him to death remain despised.

A third stratum may have something to do with this. Scholars have long recognized that the evangelists wrote with their communities in mind, a generation or two after Jesus' death—that they told their version of the Jesus story in such a way as to address their own community concerns. In this analysis, what would seem to be at the root of at least some of the anti-Jewish tone is the opposition that the first-century Christian communities faced from their longer-established Jewish brethren. It might have been easier to be more forgiving of the Jewish involvement in Jesus' death, once that death was reinterpreted, had most of the Jews not continued to reject Christianity.

Matthew's Gospel is openly anti-Jewish. On one level this is puzzling because it is also the most 'Jewish' of the four. The author was a Jew,[28] Matthew's Jesus accepts the Jewish Law as binding on his disciples, and the qualities he expects of them (e.g., learning and understanding, faith, humility, doing God's will) would have been quite acceptable to most first-century Jews. How, then, does one explain his anti-Pharisaic thrust, which culminates, in ch. 23, in the repeated invective: 'Woe to you, scribes and Pharisees, hypocrites'? And how does one explain his insistence on placing the phrase, 'His blood be on us and on our children', on the lips of the Jews (all the Jews) who accused Jesus before Pilate?

This anger also manifests itself in John's Gospel, in which 'the Jews' becomes a category that includes all those who reject God (e.g., 5.16; 8.57-59; 18.12; 19.10)[29] and are essentially unable to know God because they are children of the devil (8.44). John indirectly suggests a reason for this anger: the Christians were afraid of the Jewish authorities, who threatened their exclusion from the Jewish community. This fear is expressed first in 7.5-13. The context is an invitation to Jesus by his brothers to go up to Jerusalem during the Feast of Tabernacles in order to display his powers to all:

> For not even his brothers believed in him. Jesus said to them, 'My time has not yet come, but your time is always here. The world cannot hate you, but it hates me because I testify against it that its works are evil. Go

---

28. Traditionally, 'Matthew' was thought to be one of the twelve apostles. Even if this claim is incorrect, internal evidence strongly suggests that whoever wrote this Gospel was Jewish. For instance, the author refers to Jerusalem as the 'holy city' (4.5; 27.53), and in the Sermon on the Mount he deals with the three fundamental Jewish rituals of prayer, almsgiving, and fasting.

29. Occasionally 'the Jews' are receptive to Jesus (e.g., 11.45 when 'many of the Jews' are said to believe as a result of the raising of Lazarus), but instances of this openness are rare enough to occasion surprise.

> to the festival yourselves. I am not going to this festival, for my time has
> not yet fully come.' After saying this, he remained in Galilee. But after his
> brothers had gone to the festival, then he also went, not publicly but as it
> were in secret. The Jews were looking for him at the festival and saying,
> 'Where is he?' And there was considerable complaining about him among
> the crowds. While some were saying, 'He is a good man,' others were
> saying, 'No, he is deceiving the crowd.' Yet no one would speak openly
> about him for fear of the Jews.

The fear recurs in Joseph of Arimathea, who seeks to take Jesus' body
off the cross (19.38): 'After these things, Joseph of Arimathea, who
was a disciple of Jesus, though a secret one because of his fear of the
Jews, asked Pilate to let him take away the body of Jesus.' The basis
for this fear is stated in 12.42: people were afraid to declare their
attraction to Jesus, 'for fear that they would be put out of the
synagogue'. It is also represented in the long narration about the blind
man who is cured by Jesus (9.18-23):

> The Jews did not believe that he had been blind and had received his sight
> until they called the parents of the man who had received his sight and
> asked them, 'Is this your son, who you say was born blind? How then
> does he now see?' His parents answered, 'We know that this is our son,
> and that he was born blind; but we do not know how it is that now he
> sees, nor do we know who opened his eyes. Ask him; he is of age. He
> will speak for himself.' His parents said this because they were afraid of
> the Jews; for the Jews had already agreed that anyone who confessed
> Jesus to be the Messiah would be put out of the synagogue. Therefore his
> parents said, 'He is of age; ask him.'

John's anger against 'the Jews', therefore, emerges partly out of the
Jewish authorities' ostracism of Jews who had become Christians.
Being excluded from the Jewish community would have led to consid-
erable hardships for the Christians, for it would have entailed losing
the religious freedoms that had been granted the Jews by the Romans.
Judaism was tolerated by the Romans as an odd but relatively harmless
Eastern religion, and Christians at first were considered a Jewish sect.
This meant, among other things, that they did not have to pray
publicly to the Roman gods and were allowed to attend religious
services on the sabbath.

Placing the Johannine and Matthean anti-Judaism in context in this
manner accounts for the violent perspective, yet what remains is still
not a particularly peace-promoting model. The realization that John
considers 'the Jews' a cipher for the larger group of hostile unbelievers

may help to ease the post-holocaust conscience of some twentieth-century Christians. In a sense, however, it makes John's claims more violent, since all those outside the Christian group, both Jews and non-Jews, become the devil's brood.

Paul's letters are another example of the stark New Testament division drawn between insiders and outsiders. He does this primarily by attempting to reinforce in his communities a sense of belonging and uniqueness. The familial and affectionate terms he uses to describe the members of his churches are effective in this regard. His Christians are 'saints' or 'holy ones', the 'elect', his 'children', and the 'children of God'.[30] This insider endearment is exemplified in 1 Thess. 2.7-8:

> But we were gentle among you, like a nurse tenderly caring for her own children. So deeply do we care for you that we are determined to share with you not only the gospel of God but also our own selves, because you have become very dear to us.

Moreover, the terms 'brother' and 'sister' occur more frequently in the Pauline letters (72 times) than in any other religious corpus during the first two centuries. Paul's writings give the impression that his followers are all members of one large family beloved by God.

His use of the body metaphor also stresses the sense of belonging to one, special and living group connected to—or superimposed on—the resurrected body of Jesus. As he says to the Romans (Rom. 12.3-5):

> For by the grace given to me I say to everyone among you not to think of yourself more highly than you ought to think, but to think with sober judgment, each according to the measure of faith that God has assigned. For as in one body we have many members, and not all the members have the same function, so we, who are many, are one body in Christ, and individually we are members of one another.

In Colossians and Ephesians the metaphor is altered somewhat, with Jesus considered the head of the body, while the Christians make up

---

30. Paul uses 'saints' or 'holy ones' (*hagioi*) in Rom. 1.7; 8.27; 12.13; 15.25, 26, 31; 16.2, 15; 1 Cor. 1.2; 6.1, 2; 14.33; 16.1, 15; 2 Cor. 1.1; 8.4; 9.1, 12; 13.13; Eph. 1.1, 15, 18; 2.19; 3.8, 18; 4.12; 5.3; 6.18; Phil. 1.1; 4.21, 22; Col. 1.2, 4, 12, 26; 1 Thess. 3.13; 2 Thess. 1.10; 1 Tim. 5.10; Phlm. 5, 7; and 'elect' (*eklektos*) in Rom. 8.33; Col. 3.12; 1 Tim. 5.2; 2 Tim. 2.10; Tit. 1.1. Examples of his use of 'child' (*teknon*) include the following: (as his own children) 2 Cor. 6.13; 1 Thess. 2.7; 1 Tim. 1.2; 2 Tim. 1.2; Tit. 1.4; (as God's children) Rom. 8.16, 17, 21; 9.8; Gal. 4.28; Eph. 5.1.

the rest of that body (Col. 1.18; see also Eph. 1.22; 4.15). For Paul, participation in baptism and the Lord's supper (eucharist) provide lasting access to this body for his members.

> For just as the body is one and has many members, and all the members of the body, though many, are one body, so it is with Christ. For in the one Spirit we were all baptized into one body—Jews or Greeks, slaves or free—and we were all made to drink of one Spirit. (1 Cor. 12.12-13)

> The cup of the blessing that we bless, is it not a sharing in the blood of Christ? The bread that we break, is it not a sharing in the body of Christ? Because there is one bread, we who are many are one body, for we all partake of the one bread. (1 Cor. 10.16-17)

In fact, in each of his baptismal discourses (Gal. 3.27-28; 1 Cor. 12.12-13; Col. 3.9-11) Paul emphasizes the abolition of divisions, and exhorts all Christians to join the new 'body'.

Finally, Paul reinforces his 'in-group' by telling his members that he has access to spiritual information unknown to others, and that he can transmit that information to them. This situation, he claims, sets his communities apart from the others. In 1 Cor. 2.14–3.2 Paul explicitly states what is implicit elsewhere: he functions on the spiritual level (he has the 'mind of Christ') and can teach them much as they mature:

> Those who are unspiritual do not receive the gifts of God's Spirit, for they are foolishness to them, and they are unable to understand them because they are spiritually discerned. Those who are spiritual discern all things, and they are themselves subject to no one else's scrutiny. 'For who has known the mind of the Lord so as to instruct him?' But we have the mind of Christ. And so, brothers and sisters, I could not speak to you as spiritual people, but rather as people of the flesh, as infants in Christ. I fed you with milk, not solid food, for you were not ready for solid food.

Paul also draws the line between insiders and outsiders in another manner. He reminds his communities of the hostile people who threaten them. These he calls 'the outsiders' (1 Cor. 5.12, 13; 1 Thess. 4.12; Col. 4.5)—and, with increasing degrees of hostility, 'those who do not know God' (1 Thess. 4.5; Gal. 4.8; 2 Thess. 1.8), the 'unrighteous' (1 Cor. 6.1, 9) who are 'enemies of the cross of Christ' (Phil. 3.18) and are 'despised by the Church' (1 Cor. 6.4). He characterizes these outsiders by catalogues of vices, as 1 Cor. 9.9-11 exemplifies:

> Do you not know that wrongdoers will not inherit the kingdom of God? Do not be deceived! Fornicators, idolaters, adulterers, male prostitutes,

> sodomites, thieves, the greedy, drunkards, revilers, robbers—none of
> these will inherit the kingdom of God. And this is what some of you used
> to be. But you were justified in the name of the Lord Jesus Christ and in
> the Spirit of our Lord

At times these 'outsiders' are Christians whom Paul considers mis-guided; other times they are non-Christians. But the message remains the same: outside the Church as he conceives it lies evil.

There is a moderating feature: the boundary line was not fixed. Paul's missionary drive allowed him to see in the outsider a potential insider—either through his own hard work and the work of others, or through God's intervention. Romans 9–11 provides a fascinating example of the latter. In this section Paul struggles to understand why the Jews have not converted *en masse* to Christianity. They remain, he feels, God's chosen people, while Jesus is the long-awaited Messiah. It makes perfect sense to him. Assuming that he is right and they are wrong, he decides that it all must be part of God's plan. This leads him to speculate that, in a way, the pieces of the puzzle fit together. Had the Jews all believed in Jesus, he would have returned to initiate the end and the message would not have gone out to the others. So, he concludes, God must have prevented the Jews from believing in order to allow everyone to be saved. And God must intend to remove these blinkers from their eyes because he cannot have rejected his people. 'All Israel will be saved' (11.26) in the end, when God sees fit. Paul is too attached to his people to believe that they will be damned like all the rest (a curious double-standard here). In the meantime, though, they remain 'outsiders' and 'enemies of the church', as does the rest of humanity, including other Christians who preach a message substan-tially different from his.

Emerging clearly from Paul's letters is the belief that those who choose to reject the Christian message or the kind of Christian message preached by certain individuals fall into a different category of beings. Barring a radical change in their status, they are destined to be annihilated by God on judgment day. 'Their end is destruction', Paul insists (Phil. 3.19). The Gospels are in agreement. So too is the rest of the New Testament. Acts has Paul saying to the Jews in Corinth who resist him: 'Your blood be on your own heads!' (18.6). In some of the other letters (e.g., 1–2 Peter, 1–3 John, Jude) the insider–outsider mentality is extended to include members of these communi-ties whose actions are not in keeping with the wishes of their leaders.

The letters accuse them of the vilest acts and exclude them from the group, for there can be no middle ground. The entire brief letter of Jude is worth quoting in this regard:

Jude, a servant of Jesus Christ and brother of James, To those who are called, who are beloved in God the Father and kept safe for Jesus Christ. May mercy, peace, and love be yours in abundance.

Beloved, while eagerly preparing to write to you about the salvation we share, I find it necessary to write and appeal to you to contend for the faith that was once for all entrusted to the saints. For certain intruders have stolen in among you, people who long ago were designated for this condemnation as ungodly, who pervert the grace of our God into licentiousness and deny our only Master and Lord, Jesus Christ.

Now I desire to remind you, though you are fully informed, that the Lord, who once for all saved a people out of the land of Egypt, afterward destroyed those who did not believe. And the angels who did not keep their own position, but left their proper dwelling, he has kept in eternal chains in deepest darkness for the judgment of the great Day. Likewise, Sodom and Gomorrah and the surrounding cities, which, in the same manner as they, indulged in sexual immorality and pursued unnatural lust, serve as an example by undergoing a punishment of eternal fire.

Yet in the same way these dreamers also defile the flesh, reject authority, and slander the glorious ones. But when the archangel Michael contended with the devil and disputed about the body of Moses, he did not dare to bring a condemnation of slander against him, but said, 'The Lord rebuke you!' But these people slander whatever they do not understand and they are destroyed by those things that, like irrational animals, they know by instinct. Woe to them! For they go the way of Cain, and abandon themselves to Balaam's error for the sake of gain, and perish in Korah's rebellion. These are blemishes on your love-feasts, while they feast with you without fear, feeding themselves. They are waterless clouds carried along by the winds; autumn trees without fruit, twice dead, uprooted; wild waves of the sea, casting up the foam of their own shame; wandering stars, for whom the deepest darkness has been reserved forever.

It was also about these that Enoch, in the seventh generation from Adam, prophesied, saying, 'See, the Lord is coming with ten thousands of his holy ones, to execute judgment on all, and to convict everyone of all the deeds of ungodliness that they have committed in such an ungodly way, and of all the harsh things that ungodly sinners have spoken against him.' These are grumblers and malcontents; they indulge their own lusts; they are bombastic in speech, flattering people to their own advantage.

But you, beloved, must remember the predictions of the apostles of our Lord Jesus Christ; for they said to you, 'In the last time there will be scoffers, indulging their own ungodly lusts.' It is these worldly people, devoid of the Spirit, who are causing divisions. But you, beloved, build yourselves up on your most holy faith; pray in the Holy Spirit; keep yourselves in the love of God; look forward to the mercy of our Lord Jesus Christ that leads to eternal life. And have mercy on some who are wavering; save others by snatching them out of the fire; and have mercy on still others with fear, hating even the tunic defiled by their bodies.

Now to him who is able to keep you from falling, and to make you stand without blemish in the presence of his glory with rejoicing, to the only God our Savior, through Jesus Christ our Lord, be glory, majesty, power, and authority, before all time and now and forever. Amen.

This letter is a prime example of the violence that ensues by dividing people into groups of 'saved' and 'damned'. 'Accursed children!' the author of 2 Peter calls his similar group of dissidents (2.14). Their 'crimes' range from homosexuality to denying the full authority of the leaders. Absent is the respect for others as individuals, and as individuals who have a right to differ. Jude begins with a wish of 'peace and love' directed to the insiders, and includes no exhortation for them to inflict physical punishment on others; from our twentieth-century perspective it is one of the most violent pieces in the New Testament.

7. *Summary*

Violence abounds within the New Testament. Sometimes this fact reflects the troubles and persecutions faced by Jesus and the early Christians. Many incidents arise in which people are beaten and arrested, and some even killed (John, Jesus, Stephen, James). It is only natural that the New Testament should reflect this situation. The New Testament glorification of martyrdom adds to this presence of violence. Sometimes the violence expressed is contained in metaphors. Christians saw themselves confronting evil constantly, and they often represented their struggles through the use of military images. An extended example occurs in Eph. 6.10-17:

Finally, be strong in the Lord and in the strength of his power. Put on the whole armor of God, so that you may be able to stand against the wiles of the devil. For our struggle is not against enemies of blood and flesh, but against the rulers, against the authorities, against the cosmic powers of this present darkness, against the spiritual forces of evil in the heavenly places. Therefore take up the whole armor of God, so that you may be able to withstand on that evil day, and having done everything, to stand firm. Stand therefore, and fasten the belt of truth around your waist, and put on the breastplate of righteousness. As shoes for your feet put on

whatever will make you ready to proclaim the gospel of peace. With all of
these, take the shield of faith, with which you will be able to quench all
the flaming arrows of the evil one. Take the helmet of salvation, and the
sword of the Spirit, which is the word of God.

Sometimes the violence is linked to the New Testament's apocalyptic
basis. The texts speak repeatedly of the horrific violence soon to be
inflicted upon the earth, the battles to be fought between the forces of
God and those of Satan, and in particular the wrath of God to come
upon all non-believers. There are few pages in the New Testament
that do not reflect at least one of these forms of violence.

It is not the presence of violence that is remarkable, however, but
its promotion. The acceptable New Testament model allows for both
physical and non-physical violence to be inflicted on others. The guiding
principle concerning physical violence is that violent behaviour
is acceptable for God and Jesus when they choose, and occasionally
for humans as well. God, we are told, intervenes in the present to
'discipline' or punish people; he also allows Jesus to be killed and
Jerusalem to be destroyed, and (in Paul's opinion, according to
Romans 9–11) he 'hardens' the hearts of Jews in order to prevent
them from accepting the Christian message. Moreover, in the end time
God is expected to wage war against the forces of evil and devastate
the earth, during and after which his wrath will descend on all non-
believers. The God of the New Testament is violent. So is Jesus,
although to a lesser extent. He uses violence to 'cleanse' the temple, he
incites violence against himself and his followers by tearing families
apart and entering Jerusalem during Passover, and he is destined to
play a future role as end time judge and warrior. The New Testament
does not grant others the same liberties. Still, Christians may carry
weapons, soldiers may kill others in the line of duty and remain
Christians, Paul may threaten the members of his communities with
corporal (perhaps capital) punishment, and Peter without remorse may
lead Sapphira to her death for having lied to him. These stories and
role models legitimize the use of physical force.

The promotion of non-physical violence is even more widespread
throughout the New Testament. One way of contextualizing this point
is to explore the overall model of problem-solving Christians are
given. 'Do not insist on non-violence' is the first link to that model.
This attitude results in a situation in which problems, both personal
and institutional, do not ultimately have to be resolved peacefully. 'Do

not attempt to resolve problems now' is the second link. With the expected imminent demise of the world, the writers of the New Testament do not encourage people to change the world over time; what matters to them is the need to safeguard their audience from punishment when this world is destroyed. Little effort is made to change the societal structures that lead to various forms of violence against people. 'Do not attempt to resolve significant problems yourself' is the third link. These are left to God. The father figure is expected to take care of evil, including the Christians' enemies. This forecast effectively removes one incentive for opening constructive forms of dialogue with others. In addition, treating people as children disempowers them. 'Do not seek compromise and learning from those outside your group' is the fourth and final link. The interactive model presented by Jesus especially is one of confrontation based on the belief that he is superior. The Christian leaders, with Paul increasingly at the head, act the same way toward outsiders. They are convinced that they have the truth, whereas others, both Christian and non-Christian, do not. In this context, Christian missionary activities, endorsed by Jesus (e.g., 'Go therefore and make disciples of all the nations'—Mt. 28.19), usually violate the cultural integrity of others.

The New Testament texts insist that part of the reason for this differentiation lies in people's natures. Sometimes it is the Jews who are placed in the category of deficient beings (according to John), since they are the 'devil's children'; other times it is females, we are told, who are created inferior by God. In fact, as a Christian, one welcomes 'enemies', for the glory of martyrdom depends on others doing the killing. This attitude reflects perhaps the most serious form of violence in the New Testament: to insist that only one side is correct and that some people—in the case of the New Testament writers, the bulk of humanity—are by nature inferior, is to render lasting peace impossible.

Chapter 4

CONCLUSION

The New Testament strongly promotes peace and it strongly promotes violence. Reintroducing the image of the *trompe l'oeil*, it is like seeing in the same design either two facial profiles or a vase. One tends not to see them both simultaneously, yet each can be seen distinctively in turn. So it is with peace and violence. From one perspective the peace-promoting picture is crystal clear. 'Get along with one another' is what the New Testament authors repeat to their communities. 'Never inflict physical violence on another human being, and if you might be tempted to do so, model yourself on God who loves all of his creation. Be concerned with the welfare of others, for lasting peace includes social justice. Most importantly, strive for spiritual transformation. Once you have achieved that, the inherent value of each individual will manifest itself to you, and you will never even consider treating someone else any differently than the way you would want to be treated yourself.' From another angle the picture is transformed and violence dominates. 'Exclude from your midst those who disagree with you or dare to question your leadership', is the refrain. 'It is acceptable to impose physical violence on others, occasionally even to the point of death. Trust in God who inflicts his wrath on unbelievers. Make no effort to reform the world, for God will soon transform it, and annihilate all non-believers and false-believers. Above all, appreciate your superiority over others. The outsiders' refusal to accept your preaching is proof of their evil natures and inclinations. They will be damned and you will be saved, for salvation is only through Christ'. Both pictures are vivid. Both are fundamental to the New Testament.

How then does one make sense of the New Testament on this matter? This chapter presents some of the possibilities, which in my opinion all have their strengths and weaknesses. I have organized the discussion around two general positions. The first is that the New Testament's views on peace and violence, despite appearances to the contrary, are consistent; the second is that they are inconsistent. These positions both include a range of options. In what follows I highlight the main options available for a reasonable understanding of this corpus, giving each a fair hearing. Then I touch on how I make sense of this situation.

1. *The Views are Consistent*

Implied in this position is the belief that what appears to be incompatible in the New Testament actually reflects a unified, all-embracing understanding of reality. The peace-promoting and violence-promoting sides become complementary rather than contradictory. The most common presentation of this position holds that the New Testament simply cannot offer inconsistent views because it is inspired by God and God is consistent. Such a view, however, leads us into the realm of belief; for this reason, I leave it out of the discussion and turn instead to options which are open to rational discussion.

a. *Opposites Are Needed to Make the Whole*
One way to appreciate the polarity of opinions on peace and violence within the New Testament is to follow in the tradition of some ancient philosophical and religious systems—and, more recently, some psychoanalytical schools—that encourage individuals to recognize the presence of opposite forces within themselves. In ancient China this duality was represented by the *yin* and the *yang*, symbolized by the circle with the curving black and white halves and the white and black dots.[1] All was thought to arise out of these primal cosmic elements (*yin* representing the dark, cool, female elements; *yang*, the light, warm male elements) and all creation was thought to contain both. The human goal was not to transcend one of them, but rather to gain strength by learning how to recognize and use both. This belief in the complementarity of the male (*yang*) and female (*yin*) within each individual was adapted by C.G. Jung in our century. According to his influential psychoanalytical theory, each man has an inward, female 'face' (his *anima*) and each woman has her corresponding male side

---

1.   The classic presentation of *yin* and *yang* occurs in the Chinese divination text, *The Book of Changes*, or the *I Ching* (now transcribed *Yi Jing*).

(her *animus*). If the personality is to be healthy, the female side of the man and the masculine side of the woman must be understood and integrated.

From this perspective of complementarity, the presence of both peace-promoting and violence-promoting sides to the New Testament need not be inconsistent. On the contrary, their joint presence challenges people to integrate their violent, 'male', sides with their peaceful, 'female', sides. How consistent the New Testament message is, therefore, has less to do with the presence of two apparently opposite viewpoints than it does with its ability to allow people to grow and reach their potential as complete individuals.

b. *Mythic and Ritual Violence is Needed for People to Live in Peace*
This approach begins with the premise that all human beings have violent tendencies which, if unchecked, would make communal life impossible. To survive, we have developed over the centuries a series of checks and balances that control violence. Religions are part of this control mechanism, for violence expressed and experienced in religious myths and rituals helps to remove violence from our lives. From this perspective, the violence expressed in the New Testament, especially that attributed to God, actually serves to promote community peace. Combined with the overt injunctions to peace, the result is a uniformly peace-promoting collection.

The book of Revelation can be made to fit this perspective.[2] Reading between the lines one can reconstruct this book's historical setting without much difficulty. This small and persecuted collection of Christian communities feels rejected and scorned by Jews and non-Jews alike, frustrated by both the continued worldly successes of its critics and the delay of Jesus' final return to earth. As a result, it would like to see non-Christians brought to their knees. The author of Revelation defuses that anger in two ways. He encourages his

2.   What follows on Revelation owes much to Adela Yarbro Collins' *Crisis and Catharsis: The Power of the Apocalypse* (Philadelphia, PA: Westminster Press, 1984), especially pp. 141-63. Another perspective can be found in Leonard L. Thompson's *The Book of Revelation: Apocalypse and Empire* (New York, NY: Oxford University Press, 1990). Thompson argues that Revelation confronts apostasy more than persecution: the author's community was threatened by attraction to, and integration with, the non-Christian world, and he saw his task as painting that world as darkly as possible.

community to transfer their potential aggression to another agent (God) and another time (the End), and to reverse those aggressive feelings by demanding more of themselves. Although not everyone might agree with the means, in its own way this book is cathartic and peace-promoting.

René Girard has recently developed a comprehensive theory on the origins of religion which owes much to this viewpoint as well as to Freud's theory of religion.[3] Struck by common features in many non-literate societies, Girard hypothesizes that a single act of mob violence in primordial times (the 'founding murder') lies at the root of all religion. Over time, the communal remembering and reliving of this act, especially when directed against community-chosen scapegoats, helped to divert aggression to the outside and reinforce the stability of the socio-cultural order. Violence gave birth to religion, and religion has served to keep violence in check. The presence of violence in the religious texts and rituals, then, need not be violence-promoting.

This option is pragmatic in nature. The assumption is that all people have violent inclinations, and stories of God's wrath falling on one's enemies can sometimes be more effective in defusing anger and pro-moting peace than teachings that encourage people to 'turn the other cheek'. According to this perspective, people need both types of messages, and the New Testament serves those needs admirably and consistently.[4]

---

3.   See especially Girard's *Violence and the Sacred* (trans. P. Gregory; Baltimore, MD: The Johns Hopkins University Press, 1977 [1972]), and *The Scapegoat* (trans. Y. Freccero; Baltimore, MD: The Johns Hopkins University Press, 1986 [1982]). Girard's theory is applied more specifically to the Bible by Raymund Schwager, *Must there be Scapegoats? Violence and Redemption in the Bible* (trans. M. Assad; San Francisco, CA: Harper and Row, 1987 [1978]); J. Williams, *The Bible, Violence, and the Sacred: Liberation from the Myth of Sanctioned Violence* (New York, NY: HarperSanFrancisco, 1991); and Robert G. Hamerton-Kelly, *The Gospel and the Sacred: Poetics and Violence in Mark* (Minneapolis, PA: Fortress Press, 1994).

4.   Girard projects onto Jesus the solution for moving humanity out of the scapegoat cycle mainly through the parables that encourage people to transform themselves instead of having others solve their problems. But he does not think that Christians, including the writers of the New Testament, understood the full force of Jesus' message. By seeing something in Jesus that even his closest followers did not appreciate, and by considering Jesus to be the only religious founder to posit a way out of the cycle of violence, Girard reveals the influence of his religious bias.

2. *The Views are Inconsistent*

This position argues for the presence of an irreconcilable tension within the New Testament concerning the issue of peace and violence. Two questions naturally ensue: which factors account for this inconsistency, and how does one then interpret the New Testament message?

a. *The Contributing Factors*

The contributing factors are varied, and several no doubt explain the present situation. Four are basic. The first is the involvement of many people and communities in the composition of the New Testament books. Traditions ascribe authorship to eight individuals: Matthew, Mark, Luke (the author of the Gospel and Acts), John (the author of the Gospel, 1–3 John, and Revelation), Paul (the author of the thirteen letters in his name—and, it was thought by most, Hebrews), James, Peter (the author of 1 and 2 Peter), and Jude. Modern scholarship, besides casting doubt on knowing who actually wrote any of these documents, has significantly increased the number of authors.[5] It has also highlighted the great diversity of early Christian communities. Given the number of hands responsible for these works, consistency on all points should not be expected.

A second factor is the stretch of time during which the books were all written. Even early Christians did not claim that these documents were eyewitness accounts written two or three years after Jesus' death (in 30–33 CE). Rather, they placed Paul's letters in the 50s and 60s, Mark's Gospel in the late 60s or early 70s, and John's writings at the end of the first century. Modern scholarship has suggested that this period be extended, from 40–140 CE.[6] A fifty to one-hundred-year

5. Major differences between works ascribed to any one author in the New Testament have led to the suggestion that the author of John's gospel did not compose 1–3 John or Revelation, the author of 1 Peter did not compose 2 Peter, and several letters ascribed to Paul were not composed by him (Ephesians, Colossians, 2 Thessalonians, 1–2 Timothy, Titus—and certainly Hebrews, which is no longer regarded as belonging to the Pauline camp); tensions within individual works have led to the theory that 'schools' may have been responsible for the final versions of some works (at least John); and significant literary overlap between the Synoptic gospels has led most scholars to assume that Matthew and Luke had access to written sources which included Mark and a hypothetical document now called Q.

6. Once the apostolic authority of some of these works is doubted, the dates can be extended past the lifetimes of those associated with Jesus. 2 Peter, for instance, is

span of time certainly allows for different perspectives to enter the collection.

A third factor is the particular social situations out of which the New Testament writings emerged. First-century Christianity was made up of small groups expecting the imminent end of the world, actively engaged in convincing others of this belief. This situation certainly had an impact on what Christians wrote. The end-time focus plainly accounts for several themes (e.g., the sense of urgency, the 'all-or-nothing' stance, the acceptance of the present political order, the radical 'turn-the-other-cheek' ethic). The groups' social situation, though, may also explain some of their ideas. Mary Douglas's wide-ranging anthropological studies are of interest to us here. She argues, for instance, that 'small competitive communities tend to believe themselves to be in a dangerous universe, threatened by sinister forces'.[7] Such communities can survive by living closed existences, maintaining a high degree of internal social pressure, and expressing hostility toward cosmic powers which they perceive to be responsible for their troubles. The social settings in which the early Christians found themselves, then, might explain at least some of the authoritarianism and hostility in their writings.

Our own world-view adds a fourth contributing factor. We look at the New Testament with twentieth-century eyes. Although we certainly do not all have the same vision, as a group we bring to this corpus certain expectations and perspectives that were not there in the first century. This was an age that accepted the institution of slavery and the natural inferiority of women, the centrality of earth in the universe, and the presence of good and evil spirits influencing people's health and welfare. Moreover, to this the Jews added the belief that they were chosen by a loving, interventionist and wrathful God, who they hoped would soon intervene to destroy their enemies. At least some of this world-view is gone from present-day North America. What may strike us as inconsistent (e.g., a global peace-promoting model that ignores the equality of all humans) would not have appeared so to most people in the first century. Inconsistency often lies in the eyes of the beholder.

now often dated last (*ca*. 140 CE) because it refers to Paul's letters as 'scripture' (3.15-16), a phenomenon otherwise unattested until the mid-second century.

    7.   See especially Mary Douglas, *Natural Symbols: Explorations in Cosmology* (New York, NY: Vintage Books, 1973).

b. *The Interpretations*

The question must be faced: if the New Testament is fundamentally inconsistent when it comes to peace and violence, how is a twentieth-century reader to make sense of it? One option is simply to accept the New Testament as outdated. From this perspective, it becomes at best a well-meaning but flawed world-view no longer in tune with the value society places on human rights; at worst, it is a regressive force in the present struggle to achieve full equality and respect for all individuals in the world. Why, one might ask, should the modern world take seriously a collection of texts whose authors insist that the world will soon end (two thousand years ago!), that Jews are both God's chosen group and sons of the devil, and that women are created inferior to men by a God who has favourites, sends his son to earth to be killed, and inflicts violence on human beings at will?

Another approach is to seek a 'core' which gives the collection consistency, assuming that contingent factors have altered an otherwise coherent message. This option has two poles: one argues for a violent, the other for a peaceful core.

The first, a minority viewpoint, is based on the assumption that the writers of the New Testament did their best to cover up the 'fact' that Jesus and his followers were intent on armed revolution—and that Christian leaders for two millennia have conspired to keep the secret hidden.[8] Not surprisingly, this theory is favoured by those who wish to show that Christianity is based on fabrication. Its force emerges primarily from the question: If Jesus actually was a political revolutionary, are there historical clues that remain?

Indeed there are. His mode of death is one: our extant texts, after all, have him charged with being a revolutionary ('king' of the Jews). His entry into Jerusalem during Passover and his subsequent assault on the Temple are two other clues, for these would not be acts done by

---

8. This theory was popularized by S.G.F. Brandon's *Jesus and the Zealots: A Study of the Political Factors in Primitive Christianity* (Manchester: Manchester University Press, 1967); it is not commonly accepted by scholars because it lacks 'hard' textual evidence (and also, it must be admitted, because most New Testament scholars happen to be Christians for whom this theory creates significant personal problems). A series of rebuttals can be seen in E. Bammel and C.F.D. Moule (eds.), *Jesus and the Politics of his Day* (Cambridge: Cambridge University Press, 1984); see also Martin Hengel, *Was Jesus a Revolutionist?* (trans. W. Klassen; Philadelphia, PA: Fortress Press, 1971).

someone intent on keeping the peace. Still another is contained in the issue of whether Jews ought to pay taxes to Rome (Mk 12.13-17; Mt. 22.15-22; Lk. 20.20-26). As we saw above, this particular story gains its full force if Jesus could answer neither 'yes' nor 'no' because he had revolutionary followers who advocated rebellion against Rome. Tied to this interpretation is the observation that one of Jesus' disciples is called a 'zealot' (Lk. 6.15), a term previously linked to passionate religious devotion, associated in the mid-first century with political rebellion.[9] Then there is common sense: the early Christians would have had every reason to cover up these violent beginnings if they wished to survive in the Roman world and if they did not want to consider their founder a failed revolutionary. According to this perspective, Jesus and his early followers favoured physical violence to further their ends (they were armed, after all). They modelled themselves on God and believed that they had his support. The 'turn-the-other-cheek' attitude was superimposed on this violent core. The result is an inconsistent whole in which the message of peace, though strong, is secondary.

A far more common argument is the flip side to this conspiracy theory: the core of the New Testament message promotes peace. 'If you look at what Jesus himself really taught', is the argument, 'or even Paul—the real Paul—you will find that the focus lies on peace. Jesus stressed peace and inner transformation, and Paul showed special concern for all. He did not really consider women inferior. His true belief on this matter can be found in Gal. 3.26-28. Other statements to the contrary were either added to his authentic letters by someone else (e.g., 1 Cor. 14.34-36) or included in letters written in his name (e.g., 1 Tim. 2.9-15).' This position is favoured by Christians who believe that Jesus' 'authentic teachings' can be culled from the Gospels (scholars are divided on this issue) and that his message must have been peace-promoting because he was the Son of God.

Frequently included in this perspective is a comparison with the scenes of violence found in the Hebrew Bible. This contrast is important for Christians who consider the Hebrew Bible to be the 'Old Testament', the revealed word of God which must nevertheless be

---

9. Judas Iscariot may also fall in this category. His last name could derive from the Latin *sicarius*, or 'small dagger bearer', referring to the Jewish terrorists in the first century who tried to destabilize Roman rule of Palestine by occasionally stabbing people at random in public.

seen from the context of God's revelation in Jesus. For many interpreters, this apparent evolution in the divine message of peace—from
the 'old' message which placed more emphasis on war and a warrior
God to the 'new' one which places more emphasis on peace—is
further support for the intrinsically peace-promoting aspects of Jesus'
teachings.[10] Jesus, then, is considered the 'prince of peace', both on
the grounds of his own teachings, and in contrast to the 'Old
Testament' message. Accordingly, the New Testament view becomes,
in its heart of hearts, peace-promoting.

These basic approaches have been adopted by many who try to make
sense of the New Testament messages of peace and violence. I find
none of these approaches intellectually satisfying. The peace and
violence-promoting 'cores' certainly are more evident to others than
they are to me. I strongly suspect that the evangelists, in their urge to
turn the historical Jesus into the living Christ, presented an
unnaturally peaceful and peace-promoting image of him in their
Gospels. Yet to deduce from this—and from the mainly ambiguous
Gospel allusions to Jesus' involvement in violence—that Jesus was a
political revolutionary, whose deeds reflect a violent core that was
covered over by the evangelists, is to go further than the textual
evidence allows.[11] The violence, however, runs too deeply for me to

10. Scholars have noted that this shift away from the biblical warrior God who
leads human armies to victory is already evident within some segments of Judaism
before Jesus' time. W. Klassen expresses it well in his article, 'War in the NT', in
David Noel Freedman *et al.*, *Doubleday Anchor Bible Dictionary*, VI (New York,
NY: Doubleday, 1992), p. 869. He notes that, at least as early as the translation of
the Hebrew Bible into Greek (called the 'LXX', or 'the version of the 70 translators',
and done during the second century BCE), 'members of the Jewish community were
uneasy about portraying Yahweh as a warrior. The Hebrew prophets had already
portrayed Yahweh as a military leader of foreign nations thus breaking any idea that
Yahweh might be invoked as their exclusive military leader (Isa 42:13-16). Cyrus is
depicted as Yahweh's anointed, the instrument of righteousness... The LXX was
equally daring in taking each of the four texts in which Yahweh is described as a
"man of war" and changing them to "one who destroys war" (Exod 15:3; Isa 42:13;
Jdt 9:7; 16:3)'.

11. Sanders (*Jesus and Judaism*) adds an important point to this argument: if
Jesus and his disciples had been political revolutionaries who advocated violence
against the state, the Romans would have tracked down and killed all of Jesus'
followers after his death. That they did not do so suggests that the Romans felt no
physical threat from this messianic group.

discount it as peripheral to a 'peaceful core'. The insider–outsider perspective, the inferiority of women, the image of a violent God living in violent times are all fundamental to the New Testament message. If one must speak of a 'core' to the New Testament, it is best to see it as two-pronged.

I see little consistency in this bifurcation. Opposites may indeed be needed to form a healthy whole, as Jungian and ancient Chinese perspectives reinforce, each in their own way, but to me that does not resolve the promotion of both peace and violence in the New Testament. The same can be said of the Freudian hypothesis about a 'founding murder', repeated and sanitized by ritual violence in religious systems. To be sure, these theories can be superimposed on the New Testament to explain the presence of violence, but this can only be done by ignoring textual evidence which clearly suggests a far more complex situation. The New Testament documents speak openly of peace. The violence that I see in them for the most part would not be acknowledged by the authors themselves, who do not give the impression that they intend to encourage people to integrate both violence and peace.

When I set the New Testament documents in historical context, their lack of consistency concerning peace and violence is not surprising. We are dealing, after all, with writings which naturally reflect first-century perspectives on issues ranging from the status of women to acceptable ways of treating slaves. They emerged predominantly from communities of Jews who were convinced that Jesus' death and resurrection had ushered in a decisive new age for humanity. With this extraordinary religious belief came community expectations of the highest ethical behaviour—and daily joys and disappointments, loving bonds with community members, and ambiguous feelings about outsiders. We are also dealing with communities which, in their first hundred years, suffered many setbacks: Jesus did not return, the world continued to exist with no apparent radical changes, and fewer and fewer Jews converted to Christianity. What should surprise us perhaps is not their occasional angry outbursts and narrow-mindedness, but their ability to keep their hopes alive and project their idealism so eloquently in written form.

The authority given to the New Testament by Christians complicates matters considerably. These 27 documents were not originally prepared as 'Scripture'[12]—unlike the Qur'an or the Manichaean writings, for instance. The early Christians already had their 'Scripture'—the Jewish Bible—and it took roughly three centuries for Christian leaders to agree on a list of 27 books to complement the 'Old Testament' in an expanded Bible. Once canonized, however, these documents became authoritative, and they have helped to set ethical standards for much of the Western world. Regardless of our religious commitment, we live in a world deeply influenced by Christianity and its sacred texts. Its inconsistencies mirror and produce our inconsistencies.

How, then, do I react to the canonical New Testament's perspective on peace and violence? I find the peace-promoting side significant and still worth considering by Christians and non-Christians alike. My purpose in writing Chapter 2 was to highlight the major components of this side to the New Testament, and encourage others to consider its presence and importance. The violence-promoting side, though, is equally strong; it also disturbs me, all the more so because I rarely find it discussed in academic and non-academic circles. I wrote Chapter 3 in order to explore this 'dark side' to the New Testament, and emphasize its importance. The New Testament, I am now convinced, advocates both peace and violence. We ignore the one side or the other at our peril. This book is my attempt to share that viewpoint and also encourage others to rethink their understanding of the New Testament. I would hope that an appreciation of the New Testament's dual nature by Christians and non-Christians alike might contribute to our society's movement toward a more peaceful world, particularly given the freedom we now fortunately have to arrive at our own views on these matters. In the words again of *The Thunder: Perfect Mind* (14.18-25):

12. A possible exception to this claim is the book of Revelation, which closes as follows (22.18-19): 'I warn everyone who hears the words of the prophecy of this book: if anyone adds to them, God will add to that person the plagues described in this book; if anyone takes away from the words of the book of this prophecy, God will take away that person's share in the tree of life and in the holy city, which are described in this book.' Ironically, many Christians until the mid-fourth century did not consider this book 'inspired'. For information about this historical detail, and others concerning the canonization of the New Testament, see: Harry Y. Gamble, *The New Testament Canon: Its Making and Meaning* (Philadelphia, PA: Fortress Press, 1985); and Bruce M. Metzger, *The Canon of the New Testament: Its Origin, Development and Significance* (Oxford: Clarendon Press, 1987).

You who deny me, confess me,
and you who confess me, deny me.
You who tell the truth about me, lie about me,
and you who have lied about me, tell the truth about me.
You who know me, be ignorant of me,
and those who have not known me, let them know me.

BIBLIOGRAPHY

Bainton, R., *Christian Attitudes to War and Peace* (Nashville, TN: Abingdon Press, 1960).

Bammel, E., and C.F.D. Moule (eds.), *Jesus and the Politics of his Day* (Cambridge: Cambridge University Press, 1984).

Brandon, S.G.F., *Jesus and the Zealots: A Study of the Political Factors in Primitive Christianity* (Manchester: Manchester University Press, 1967).

Brown, R.M., *Religion and Violence* (Philadelphia, PA: The Westminster Press, 2nd edn, 1987 [1973]).

Brownlee, W.H., 'From Holy War to Holy Martyrdom', in H.B. Huffmon, F.A. Spina and A.R.W. Green (eds.), *The Quest for the Kingdom of God: Studies in Honour of George Mendenhall* (Winona Lake, IN: Eisenbrauns, 1983), pp. 281-92.

Edwards, G., *Jesus and the Politics of Violence* (New York, NY: Harper & Row, 1972).

Furnish, V.P., 'War and Peace in the New Testament', *Interpretation* 38 (1984), pp. 363-79.

Girard, R., *Violence and the Sacred* (trans. P. Gregory; Baltimore, MD; The Johns Hopkins University Press, 1977 [1972]).

Gutiérrez, G., *A Theology of Liberation* (Maryknoll, NY: Orbis Books, 1972).

Hamerton-Kelly, R.G., *The Gospel and the Sacred: Poetics and Violence in Mark* (Minneapolis, PA: Fortress Press, 1994).

Hengel, M., *Was Jesus a Revolutionist?* (trans. W. Klassen; Philadelphia, PA: Fortress Press, 1971).

—*Victory over Violence: Jesus and the Revolutionists* (Philadelphia, PA: Fortress Press, 1973).

Hornus, J.-M., *It is Not Lawful for me to Fight: Early Christian Attitudes towards War, Violence and the State* (trans. A. Kreider and O. Coburn; Scottsdale, PA: Herald Press, 1980 [1960]).

Jewett, R., *The Captain America Complex: The Dilemma of Zealous Nationalism* (Santa Fe, NM: Bear and Company, 2nd edn, 1984 [1973]).

Klassen, W., '"A Child of Peace" (Luke 10.6) in First Century Context', *New Testament Studies* 27 (1981), pp. 488-506.

—*Love of Enemies: The Way to Peace* (Overtures to Biblical Theology, 15; Philadelphia, PA: Fortress Press, 1984).

—'"Peace" and "War in the New Testament"', in D.N. Freedman *et al.* (eds.), *The Doubleday Anchor Bible Dictionary* (New York, NY: Doubleday, 1992), V, pp. 206-12, and VI, pp. 867-75.

Marshall, I.H., 'New Testament Perspectives on War', *The Evangelical Quarterly* 57 (1985), pp. 115-32.

Mott, S.C., *Biblical Ethics and Social Change* (New York, NY: Oxford University Press, 1982).

Richardson, P., *Paul's Ethic of Freedom* (Philadelphia, PA: The Westminster Press, 1979).

Rudolph, K. *Gnosis: The Nature and History of Gnosticism* (trans. R. Mcl. Wilson; San Francisco: Harper and Row, 1983 [1975]).

Schüssler-Fiorenza, E. *In Memory of her: A Feminist Theological Reconstruction of Christian Origins* (New York, NY: Crossroad, 1983).

Schwager, R., *Must there be Scapegoats? Violence and Redemption in the Bible* (trans. M.L. Assad; San Francisco, CA: Harper and Row, 1987 [1978]).

Sider, Ronald J., *Christ and Violence* (Scottsdale, PA: Herald Press, 1979).

Stevens, B.A., 'The Divine Warrior in the Gospel of Mark', *Biblische Zeitschrift* 31 (1987), pp. 101-11.

Swartley, W.M., *Slavery, Sabbath, War, and Women: Case Issues in Biblical Interpretation* (Scottsdale, PA: Herald Press, 1983).

Swartley, W.M., 'Politics and Peace (*Eirene*) in Luke's Gospel', in J. Cassidy and P.J. Sharper (eds.), *Political Issues in Luke–Acts* (Maryknoll, NY: Orbis Books, 1983), pp. 18-37.

Tambasco, A.J. (ed.), *Blessed are the Peacemakers: Biblical Perspectives on Peace and its Social Foundations* (New York, NY: Paulist Press, 1989).

Wengst, K., *Pax Romana and the Peace of Jesus Christ* (trans. J. Bowden; Philadelphia, PA: Fortress Press, 1987 [1986]).

Williams, J.G., *The Bible, Violence, and the Sacred: Liberation from the Myth of Sanctioned Violence* (New York, NY: HarperSanFrancisco, 1991).

Wink, W., *Engaging the Powers: Discernment and Resistance in a World of Domination* (Philadelphia, PA: Fortress Press, 1992).

Yoder, J.H., *The Politics of Jesus* (Grand Rapids, MI: Eerdmans, 1972).

Zerbe, G., *Non-Retaliation in Early Jewish and New Testament Texts: Ethical Themes in Social Contexts* (Journal for the Study of the Pseudepigrapha Supplement Series, 13; Sheffield: JSOT Press, 1993).

INDEXES

INDEX OF REFERENCES

OLD TESTAMENT

NEW TESTAMENT

Peace, Violence and the New Testament

OTHER ANCIENT SOURCES

INDEX OF AUTHORS

THE BIBLICAL SEMINAR